Sensational

BRIGHT LIGHTS, RED LIGHTS, MURDERS, GHOSTS & GARDENS

Victoria

by EVE LAZARUS

2nd Printing: April 2013.

Library and Archives Canada Cataloguing in Publication

Lazarus, Eve
    Sensational Victoria : bright lights, red lights, murders, ghosts & gardens / Eve Lazarus.

Includes bibliographical references and index.
ISBN 978-1-927380-06-2

1. Victoria (B.C.)–History–Anecdotes. 2. Victoria (B.C.)–Biography–Anecdotes.
I. Title.

FC3846.4.L39 2012   971.1'28   C2012-905494-1

Cover design: Rayola Graphic Design
Interior design: Derek von Essen
Maps by Ross Nelson
Cover photo credits:
(top) The roof of the BC Legislature, Victoria; Empress Hotel in the distance. Royal BC Museum, image #I-03081
(bottom, L to R) Alice Munro, David Foster (centre), Bruce Hutchison, Nellie McClung
Back cover photo credits:
(clockwise from top left) Nellie McClung, Stella Carroll, Mabel Fortune Driscoll, Emily Carr House, 132 South Turner Street (1889), Pat Martin Bates, Captain Leonard Locke

Represented in Canada by the Literary Press Group.

Distributed in Canada by the University of Toronto Press and in the U.S. by Small Press Distribution (SPD).

The publisher gratefully acknowledges the financial assistance of the Canada Council for the Arts, the Canada Book Fund, and the Province of British Columbia through the B.C. Arts Council and the Book Publishing Tax Credit.

Anvil Press Publishers Inc.
P.O. Box 3008, Main Post Office
Vancouver, B.C. V6B 3X5 Canada
www.anvilpress.com

Printed and bound in Canada

FOR MIKE

ACKNOWLEDGEMENTS

It would be impossible to write a regional history book without the assistance of the province's archives, museums, and public libraries. Special thanks to Kelly-Ann Turkington at BC Archives, Sarah Rathjen at the City of Victoria Archives, Sherri Robinson and Greg Evans at Esquimalt Archives, Jean Sparks at Oak Bay Archives, Caroline Posynick, archivist at Royal Roads University, Sonia Nicholson and Evelyn Wolfe at Saanich Archives, Talonbooks, Deirdre Castle at the *Times Colonist*, Nada Lora, University of Victoria's McPherson Archives, Karen Wallis and Detective Jonathan Sheldan at the Victoria Police Department.

I was very fortunate to be able to draw on the resources of a prolific bunch of reporters, authors, and historians who have amassed a formidable body of work about Victoria. Although I have included a detailed bibliography, special thanks to the Victoria Heritage Foundation for its wonderful series of This Old House books, and to John Adams, Robert Amos, Paul Chamberlain, Ruth Copley, Jeff de Jong, Patrick Dunae, Linda Eversole, Cornelia Lange, Joan Looy, Ross Nelson, Jan Ross, and Steve Webb who all generously gave me their time and expert assistance.

Sincere thanks to the relatives and the dozens of homeowners, past and current, who shared their personal stories with me, loaned me family photos, and let me into their homes. You'll meet them in the pages of this book.

I'm especially grateful to my publisher Brian Kaufman for sharing my enthusiasm for this project. Special thanks to my editor Maureen Nicholson, to book designer Derek von Essen, Clint Hutzulak for his wonderful cover design, and to Karen Green and Caroline McGechaen at Anvil Press.

PREFACE

My obsession with old houses and their stories started in 2002. I was planning a trip to Australia and discovered a 1970 biography of my aunt Joan Rosanove. The book gave the address of the house where my father was born in Ballarat and had an intriguing paragraph. My grandmother Ruby Lazarus, who died years before I was born, was apparently more than a little eccentric and made some strange modifications to her house.

The house was a typical Australian Victorian, with bedrooms and living areas off a central hallway. It was painted mud yellow and sat behind a picket fence of the same colour. Cast-iron lacework decorated the front of the house and ran along a verandah supported by fluted iron pillars. The current owners let me look around, and I filled them in on 30 years of their home's social history. They'd raised five children in the house, and thanks to the book and Ruby, I was able to solve the 25-year mystery of why a number of doors led nowhere. Apparently, as each of Ruby's eight children moved away, she had their bedrooms lopped off the house. I could never find out why.

Around the same time, I met James Johnstone. James runs Home History Research Services from his Strathcona home and is a kind of "house detective" who uncovers the social history of houses, including everyone who ever lived there, whether the house was once a funeral parlour or a brothel, and the context of the house in the neighbourhood. I found other home researchers across the country. I was hooked.

I wrote a series of magazine and newspaper articles about the histories and mysteries behind various houses across Canada, published *At Home with History: The Untold Secrets of Greater Vancouver's Heritage Homes* (Anvil Press, 2007), and started a weekly blog at www.evelazarus.com/blog.

A book on Victoria, with the city's history, gorgeous houses, and eccentricities, seemed a natural next step. The most time consuming part was deciding which stories to include and then putting them in context. Sometimes the context decided the story. On several occasions, I'd visit homeowners to talk about their heritage garden or some famous person who had lived in their house, and would come away with a ghost, a madam, or a murder story that changed the structure of the book.

In 1907, the City of Victoria replaced its old and confusing way of numbering buildings and naming streets, and that year many buildings were renumbered and street names changed. People also moved frequently and it was sometimes difficult to figure out if the house fit the story. Nell Shipman's house was particularly challenging, and its location is still a best guess after my searching through city directories, dating the houses through the architecture, looking at maps, and pacing the streets.

All of the houses in the book still stand—or at least they did when I finished the research—and they range from fabulous mansions to ordinary cottages. This book is all about their stories, because I'm convinced that social history is every bit as important as architectural history in preserving buildings for future generations.

Much of the research for this book came from the city directories, the Census, and Vital Events records. I scoured heritage inventories, old newspapers, the Victoria Public Library's murder files, and a huge amount of online resources, including the archives of the *Times Colonist* (1858 to 1910).

Most valuable of all were the personal recollections of current homeowners, as well as those of past homeowners and, in many cases, their descendants.

INTRODUCTION

Emily Carr figures prominently in the book. That wasn't intentional. Many excellent books have been written about her, and she is already so well known I hadn't planned to feature her in *Sensational Victoria*. But she kept getting in my head and turning up in the most unlikely places. My niece Stephanie Dunn first told me about Emily's Oak Bay cabin. Her husband, Patrick, knew somebody who knew somebody else who put me on to Terri Tallentire, who came to the rescue of Emily's cabin in 1995. I was even more intrigued when I couldn't find any reference to the cabin in Emily's own books and memoirs, and only the odd mention in books written about her.

Emily would also pop up unexpectedly in connection to people in unrelated chapters in this book. Today, Emily is a regular, for instance, on John Adams's popular ghost tours, and I was intrigued by how many James Bay houses had figured in her life. After I met Jan Ross at Carr House and read about Cezanne's walking tour of Provence, my idea became to discover what James Bay would have been like a hundred years ago through the eyes of the 42-year-old artist.

In some ways, Emily is the string that pulls this book together. Her walking tour, told in my first chapter, was an obvious segue into "Five Legendary Women of Victoria." This chapter was a tough one to narrow down, and I chose Emily Carr, Nellie McClung, Gwen Cash, Sylvia Holland, and Capi Blanchet, because they are smart, fearless women who made a difference and lived in interesting houses that still stand today.

So much of Victoria's history is about the sea that it seemed natural to continue in the third chapter, "Tales of the Sea," with stories of the adventurers who figured in the literature of the time: explorers, a rum-runner, and a survivor of the sinking of the *Titanic*. And, where there are sailors, there are brothels, as detailed in the fourth chapter, "Victoria's Red Light District." Victoria had one of the bigger and better-run red light districts in North America. Many of the city's most respectable citizens frequented Victoria's brothels, several owned a stake in or rented out buildings to madams, and many of the working girls at these high-end establishments were to marry into respectable families.

Like any city, Victoria also has had its share of murders, and these stories span more than a century. Perhaps some of these victims have returned to haunt the city. The fifth and sixth chapters tell these tales.

As well as being the most haunted city in BC, Victoria is known as the City of Gardens, many of which are attached to heritage houses. Although Butchart Gardens is the city's number one tourist attraction, I have concentrated in the seventh chapter on the lesser-known gardens and, thanks to the generosity of their owners, several spectacular private gardens.

The next two chapters—"Bright Lights" and "The Limners"—started off as a single chapter featuring the houses of some talented people who originated in the city. But there were just too many. The stories kept growing and my problem was keeping it to just two chapters. I've selected the houses that have the best stories and are just the most fun. I spent an amazing afternoon with Pat Martin Bates in her incredible house, and one of the nicest emails I received was from David Foster, who asked me if I could include more information about his six wonderful sisters in the story of his childhood home.

The final chapter suggests a stroll around Victoria, with an emphasis on the heritage buildings that reflect the city's history.

All of the homeowners, past and present, are fiercely proud of their homes. They are the custodians—sometimes for just a few years, other times for decades—who add their own stories to the homes and in turn play a vital part in the ongoing history of *Sensational Victoria*.

CHAPTER 1

In the Steps of Emily Carr

Emily Carr is Canada's answer to the renowned Georgia O'Keeffe. Emily's name adorns a university, a school, a bridge, and a library. She is the subject of several documentaries, museum exhibits, books, and plays. In 2009, a Carr oil painting sold for more than $2.1 million, making *Wind in the Tree Tops* one of the highest-priced Canadian paintings ever sold at auction. Tourists visit her family home, seek out her sketching places along Dallas Road and Beacon Hill Park, and walk over the memorial bridge paid for by her sister Alice. Her grave is the most sought-after in the Ross Bay Cemetery.

Jan Ross, who runs Carr House, says about 12,000 people visit the house every year.

Emily's presence in Victoria is pervasive. Yet for most of her life, she was shunned by the Victoria of her day, and for all of her fame, locals still seem a bit stunned by the attention. It wasn't until the fall of 2010—65 years after her death—that Victoria honoured the artist with a $400,000 statue on the lawn of the Fairmont Empress Hotel.

Emily was born at Carr House in 1871 and died a few blocks away, 74 years later. For most of her life, she lived in James Bay and wrote extensively about the area and her family's homes in *The Book of Small*, *The House of All Sorts*, and *Hundreds and Thousands*.

JAMES BAY
James Bay is the oldest residential area of Victoria and takes its name from Governor James Douglas. Douglas built his house in the 1850s on the current site of the Royal BC Museum.

In 1863, Richard Carr, a successful wholesale merchant, bought several acres of what was once the Hudson's Bay Company–run Beckley Farm and built his home. As a young girl, Emily would walk her father partway to his warehouse on Wharf Street. They'd ramble along the planked sidewalks of Carr Street, past picket fences and wild roses, watching for horses pulling carts and for carriages trundling along the dirt road. When they reached Toronto Street, they'd turn left and skirt the

The Carr family, 207 Government St. 1869 IMAGE C-03805 ROYAL BC MUSEUM, BC ARCHIVES

11

edges of Mrs. McConnell's cow farm. They'd pass by Mrs. Fraser's Marifield Cottage, where Emily spent her early school years, then turn up Princess (now Heather) Street to continue on Michigan Street until they reached Birdcage Walk, the continuation of Carr Road.

Until a causeway was completed in the early 1900s, Government Street was made up of Carr Street (named after Richard), Birdcage Walk, and the James Bay Bridge—a wooden bridge that crossed the mud flats and continued downtown.

In 1908, the James Bay mud flats were hidden underneath the spanking-new, $13-million Empress Hotel. A bridge spanned Government Street and the city's population was close to 68,000.

By the 1940s, houses had taken over all the land. Postwar development hit in the 1950s, and then in the 1960s and '70s, many of Victoria's superb heritage houses were bulldozed to make way for apartment buildings.

Yet even with all these changes, the Victoria Heritage Foundation still lists over 150 buildings on its heritage inventory, some dating back to the 1850s.

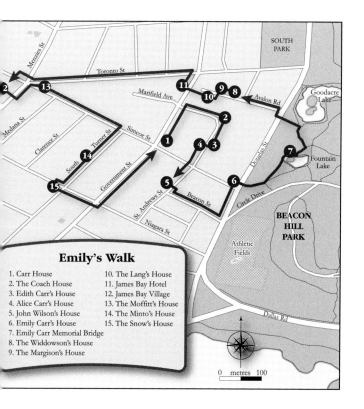

Emily's Walk

1. Carr House
2. The Coach House
3. Edith Carr's House
4. Alice Carr's House
5. John Wilson's House
6. Emily Carr's House
7. Emily Carr Memorial Bridge
8. The Widdowson's House
9. The Margison's House
10. The Lang's House
11. James Bay Hotel
12. James Bay Village
13. The Moffitt's House
14. The Minto's House
15. The Snow's House

0   metres   100

A 1913 WALKING TOUR

After years spent studying art in San Francisco, London, and Paris, Emily Carr, 42, returned to Victoria to find her birth city in a state of collapse. Page after page of ads from realty and investment companies, homes for sale, and companies offering everything from flooring and doors to sashes and windows crammed Henderson's 1913 city directory. But the truth was that the bottom had fallen out of the real estate market. Investment sources dried up as events in Europe spiralled toward World War I, building had all but stopped, unemployment rose, and the city found itself in the middle of a province-wide Depression.

1) Carr House: 207 Government Street (ca. 1863)
Richard Carr had died in 1888 and left his five daughters $50,000 and what was left of the original property. By 1913, the capital was mostly depleted and his acreage cut into city lots and divided among the Carr sisters.

Emily turned down the driveway of Carr House and glanced back at the family home designed by Wright and Sanders, the architects of the Fisgard Lighthouse in Esquimalt Harbour. Made from California redwood, the chimneys of California brick, and the mantelpieces of black marble, the house for many years was the only one on the east side of the street between Simcoe and Toronto.

Emily turned again and walked up Government Street. Hedgerows still lined the roads, but now houses popped up where once there were only cows and paddocks, fields, and orchards. She looked down the Cridges' long driveway, filled with laurels and roses, toward the house where Bishop Cridge had recently died, aged 96. The bishop's house survived until the late 1920s, when it was demolished and his driveway became Marifield Avenue.

2) 247 St. Andrews Street (ca. 1899)

Emily walked down St. Andrews Street. William and Lillian Maddock had moved into the small house in 1899 and worked at Castlewood, the mansion at the corner of Douglas Street and Avalon Road. William Maddock was a gardener and labourer who worked for William G. Bowman, first owner of Castlewood and proprietor of the Metropolitan Livery Stables on Yates Street. By 1903, his new boss was Lieutenant Colonel John A. Hall, a director of the Victoria Chemical Company. By 1911, Hall had sold the property to Stephen Jones, owner of the Dominion Hotel. Jones lived in the house until 1943, when it was torn down to make way for the Bickerton Court apartment high-rise.

John Wilcox and his new bride, Judith, bought the coach house in the early 1970s. While doing work on the house, Wilcox found several old Chinese coins buried in the dirt under the front steps. "On occasion my wife and I heard what sounded like footsteps on the stairs leading to the top floor when we duplexed part of the home," he says. "There was definitely no one at home in that part of the house when we heard these sounds."

(above) Built at the end of the 19th century, the Coach House was once on the grounds of Castlewood, a mansion at Douglas Street and Avalon Road. PHOTO COURTESY JOHN WILCOX, CA.1970

(below) Built in 1863, the childhood home of Emily Carr is now a national historic site. EVE LAZARUS PHOTO

The spirits had left by the time Martin and Jackie Somers bought the house from the Wilcoxes in 1974. "What you see from St. Andrews is actually originally the back of the house," says Jackie Somers. "When we renovated the house in the '70s, we uncovered the original coach house doors in the wall now facing the Bickerton Court parkade."

3) 231 St. Andrews Street (1913)

In 1913, Emily's oldest sister, Edith, 57, completed a large Edwardian four-square on her share of the Carr property, a few houses down from the Maddocks'. She and their sister Lizzie, 46, lived in the house for two years before moving back to the family home on Carr Street.

4) 218–220 St. Andrews Street (ca. 1903)

Emily's sister Alice, 44, lived in the Edwardian cottage at the back of Carr House and built on the site of the family's former vegetable garden. The yellow cottage had belonged to the gardener before Alice, a schoolteacher, moved her home and classroom here from 617 Battery Street.

In 1913, Bruce Hutchison was 12. The future journalist and author had learned to read and write in Alice's single-room kindergarten, as did his daughter years later in the same room and by the same methods. "Alice, a brisk, chirpy little spinster, enforced strict discipline, and allowed white doves to flutter about her schoolroom," Hutchison writes in *The Far Side of the Street*. "Amid these distractions she finally taught me to read and write, a considerable feat at my age of eight."

Hutchison describes Emily as a "dowdy, dumpy woman" with many pet animals, including a monkey riding on her shoulder. "The world of art remembers her as Victoria's only true genius and perhaps the only painter of any nation who could understand and paint the rain forest," he writes.

Years later, and shortly before her death in 1945, Emily would move into a separate flat at the back of Alice's house and teach art classes there in the studio. Alice continued to live in the house until she died at 85 in 1953.

In 1913, Emily borrowed $5,000 from Alice to build a boarding house where she could live, paint, and earn some income from her share of the land. As in most days that summer, she planned to watch over the building of her house on her share of the Carr property's former cow pasture.

Today, though, she continued down St. Andrews Street past John Wilson's house at 136 St. Andrews, thinking that if she'd spent more time studying his own rather ordinary house, she might have decided to pick an architect who better fit her personality and listened to her ideas.

5) 136 St. Andrews Street (ca. 1912)

On the recommendation of her family, Emily had hired John Wilson to design her boarding house. It was a terrible decision and they fought from the beginning.

Emily eventually got her revenge by immortalizing the relationship in *The House of All Sorts*. She describes Wilson as a "querulous, dictatorial man who antagonized his every workman." She explains how she sketched out a plan of the house and asked the architect for a cost estimate. "He returned my drawing so violently elaborated that I did not recognize it. I said, 'But this is not the house I want.'" Wilson told her she would have to pay him $200 whether she accepted the plan or not. "I was too inexperienced to fight. I knew nothing about house building ... I could not afford to pay another architect as well as this one for his wretched plan. It seemed there was nothing to do but go on."

Emily turned east along Beacon and walked up Douglas to Simcoe Street.

(opposite/top) Edith Carr built this house on her share of the Carr property in 1913. EVE LAZARUS PHOTO

(opposite/bottom) Alice Carr's house was built on the family's vegetable garden and originally belonged to the gardener. EVE LAZARUS PHOTO

(below) John Wilson's house. EVE LAZARUS PHOTO

6) The House of All Sorts: 646 Simcoe Street (1913)

Emily called her large, two-storey British Arts and Crafts home "Hill House," but it became known as The House of All Sorts after the different characters who boarded there. The house is still privately owned and maintained as a fourplex and has a national heritage designation. There are two large Indian eagles that Emily painted on the ceiling of the attic where she slept. Their wings cover the entire ceiling.

"From the front of the house you got no hint that it contained the finest studio in the town," she writes. When she needed more room in the second-floor studio, Emily suspended chairs from the ceiling, each with its own pulley system, and she would lower them to the floor as she needed them.

The second-floor studio has a row of five casement windows that look out onto Beacon Hill Park. It had a view of the Park Tea Rooms, opened in 1912 at the corner of Simcoe and Douglas. In 1864, Richard Carr had sold an acre of land to Mrs. Lusch on condition that she never turn it into a pub. Mrs. Lusch, being a little short on ethics, opened the Park Hotel as soon as the ink was dry on the deal.

An ad that year in the *British Colonist* called the hotel "a delightful retreat, fitted up regardless of expense for the comfort and accommodation of the public." Emily called it "one of the horridest saloons in Victoria … the wicked old Park Hotel roaring its tipsy trade." The pub changed hands and name, becoming the Colonist Hotel, and by 1912 it had morphed into the Park Tea Rooms and operated as that business until the early 1920s.

Emily owned The House of All Sorts for 23 years.

7) Emily Carr Memorial Bridge, Beacon Hill Park (1952)

After spending a frustrating hour watching her architect argue with his contractor, Emily crossed Douglas Street and walked along the outskirts of Beacon Hill Park, one of her favourite places to stroll and to sketch. She passed a spot where in 1952 a small stone bridge would be designed by A.R. Hennell and dedicated to her memory by her sister Alice.

Emily sat in the park for a while, then crossed back over Douglas and headed up Avalon Street, where a small subdivision had popped up along Avalon and Phoenix Place (now Huntington), with houses owned by a dentist, a contractor, a barber, a pharmacist, a printer, and a carpenter.

8) 624 Avalon Street (1904)

Emily waved to Christina Widdowson, who was working in her garden with her husband, Fred, a lamp trimmer with the city electrical light plant. Their home is one of thousands of Edwardian Vernacular Arts and Crafts that went up in Victoria between 1904 and 1914.

What's interesting about this house is that the owners only discovered in 2009 that it had been designed by the highly regarded architect Samuel Maclure. That's when Sandra McMillan, Christina and Fred's great-great-granddaughter, dropped by. Sandra's grandmother Marilyn McMillan had lived in the house when she was a child and still has the original blueprint with Maclure's signature. The Maclures lived nearby on Superior Street until 1905.

Laura West has lived in the house since 1975, and like Christina Widdowson before her, she spends a lot of time in her garden. Many former residents have visited. "I've had people come by and say they remember playing on the floor in the kitchen," she says. "A couple came by who live in California now and they said they'd started their marriage here in an upstairs suite. Another fellow dropped by with a picture from when he lived here in the '40s."

9) 614 Avalon Street (1908)

John and Lydia Margison likely named their Edwardian Vernacular Arts and Crafts house "Withernsea" after a town in Yorkshire, England. John, a well-known football player, co-founded Margison Brothers Printers on Wharf Street. The house stayed in the family until Lydia died in 1969 at age 84.

Fiona Gilsenan, a writer and book editor from California, bought the house in 2002 and lived there for five years with her husband and two children. "I just totally fell in love with the house," she says, adding that the wisteria that still frames the front of the house is the same one she saw in an archival photo from the 1920s. "It was funny how many people I ran into over the years who had lived in that house." The most famous connection she met was Richard Margison, the original owner's grandson and now a world-famous opera singer.

"I met him once when he gave a concert here in Victoria," she says. "He told me his father was born in the front bedroom." That bedroom was also Gilsenan's young daughter's room, and at one time the room had a big dragon she painted on the ceiling.

10) 613 Avalon Street (1890)

This quirky Queen Anne cottage is one of the oldest houses on the street, built by William Lang for $2,100. Lang called the cottage "Rose Thorp" and put in gingerbread detailing, bow windows, a widow's walk along the roof, unusual angles, and surprising shapes and colours—all to show off his design and building skills.

(top) A recent photo of the Widdowson's house. EVE LAZARUS PHOTO

(bottom) William Lang built Rose Thorp in 1890 to show off his design and building talents. EVE LAZARUS PHOTO

11) James Bay Hotel: 270 Government Street (1911)

Emily walked down Avalon to the James Bay Hotel, constructed two years earlier on property originally owned by Bishop Cridge. The hotel is the third oldest in Victoria, designed by architect Charles Elwood Watkins and built by the Parfitt brothers. Mother Cecilia's religious order bought the building in 1942, and it was here where Emily died in 1945, a block from where she was born.

Today the building is known as the James Bay Inn. Emily would be mortified to learn that the room in which she passed her last days is now the men's room of the pub.

12) James Bay Village

Continuing along Government Street, Emily turned west on Toronto to the Five Corners intersection at Simcoe Street and what is the historic and present-day centre of James Bay Village.

(above left) The James Bay Hotel is the third oldest hotel in Victoria. PHOTO CA.1914, CITY OF VICTORIA ARCHIVES MO9153

(above right) Mother Cecilia bought the hotel in 1942 and ran it as St. Mary's Priory. It was here that Emily Carr died in 1945. EVE LAZARUS PHOTO

(bottom) In 1913 this restaurant was the home of Robert Moffitt, a blacksmith, and his family. EVE LAZARUS PHOTO

13) The Bent Mast: 512 Simcoe Street (1884)

The Bent Mast is now a restaurant in the heart of the village. In the 1880s, the house was owned by James Angus. His daughter Mary married Benjamin Tingley Rogers, Vancouver's first millionaire industrialist and the owner of the BC Sugar Refinery. After the Angus family moved to Rockland in 1890, the house became in turn a rooming house, a brothel, four different restaurants, and an erotic art gallery.

In 1913, Robert Moffitt, a blacksmith, and his family lived here.

Apparently, a number of ghosts haunt The Bent Mast. According to the back of the restaurant menu, there's a happy child, a cranky old man who likes to hide things in the kitchen, and an older, "motherly-looking" woman who was first seen on the stairwell and upstairs, and has since been sighted on the main floor and standing on the back porch looking back into the kitchen.

19

14) 132 South Turner Street (1889)

Leaving the ghosts behind, Emily walked east along Simcoe and turned down South Turner Street. She strolled past a number of houses built between the late 1800s and the early 1900s. Several of these houses still stand, and likely the most photographed one is this colourful Queen Anne. Derek Hawksley, a set builder, and Maureen MacIntosh, a prop builder, bought the rundown house in 1984, with its false ceilings and some really bad renovations tacked on over the years.

"When we bought it, the walls and the floors were all going in different directions. We signed the papers on the table in the living room, and I put down the pen and it rolled right off," Derek says. "We both decided it's the kind of place you'd want to come home to."

Skene Lowe and James Hall, two well-known early Victoria photographers, had built the house as a rental property before selling it to Alexander and Elizabeth McMorran in 1907. The McMorrans' grandson Eric owned McMorran's Beach House until 2010, a business he'd started in 1919 with his father in Cordova Bay. In 1913 John Minto, *Times* editor lived here.

Derek spent years researching the history of his house and found through the city directories that nearly 100 people had lived there. He has two archival pictures of his house—one taken in the 1890s and another taken in the early 1900s that he found stuffed in his mailbox one day. He was able to identify one of the men as a gardener at Butchart Gardens. It sparked an immediate connection for Derek, who had also spent a number of years working at Butchart Gardens in charge of fireworks.

15) 570 Niagara Street (1908)

As Emily continued along South Turner and turned down Niagara Street, she stopped to look at the Edwardian Arts and Crafts house on the corner, built in 1908 and rented to Isaac Snow, a carpenter. A century later, the garden of this house is filled with sculptures created by owner Birgit Piskor and nestled in a garden filled with colour. The house, as Emily would have noted in 1913, sits on the former manure pile of Beckley Farm, less than two blocks from her birth-place and the start of the tour.

CHAPTER 2

Five Legendary Women of Victoria

Emily Carr is one of a number of gutsy women in Victoria who grew up or arrived in the city in the late 1800s and early 1900s. The only one of these women not to marry, Emily struggled financially perhaps more than the others, but all five women lived their lives creatively and independently at a time when women were actively discouraged from doing so. They took very different paths from those prescribed by society.

Whether they created their art in a new direction, fought for the rights of all women, or broke into traditionally male fields, they remained true to themselves as they documented and changed our world.

(opposite) Emily Carr, age 22 in 1893. IMAGE H-02813 ROYAL BC MUSEUM, BC ARCHIVES

(left) Emily Carr's Oak Bay cottage after it was moved to its new location on Foul Bay Road. COURTESY OAK BAY ARCHIVES

EMILY CARR (1871—1945)
Oak Bay Cottage

One sunny June morning in 1995, Terri Tallentire watched as workers loaded Emily Carr's cottage onto the back of a Nickel Bros. house-moving truck. Terri handed out glasses of champagne, while friends and neighbours lined the streets to take photos. One woman passed out fresh strawberries and grapes. Another played the accordion. A banner wrapped around the cottage said *For Emily. For Heritage*.

Workers from the moving company sat on top of the cottage twisting telephone wires and lifting oak branches out of the way. The truck inched carefully and slowly to the Tallentires' Oak Bay house about 10 blocks away where the cottage would take up residence as a private art studio.

Built in 1913, Emily Carr's Oak Bay cottage was saved from demolition in 1995.
EVE LAZARUS PHOTO

Roger and Terri Tallentire paid $1 to the owners of 494 Victoria Avenue for the historic cottage. They paid another $4,000 to have it moved to their property, saving the tiny structure from obliteration.

Emily started writing in the late 1920s and had seven books published during her lifetime and after her death. She wrote extensively about James Bay and her family home in *The Book of Small*, about her time as a landlady in *The House of All Sorts*, and about selling that house, her family home, and her later houses in *Hundreds and Thousands*. Yet with all these books, including her autobiography, there is not one mention of the Oak Bay cottage.

Probably the cottage was a much-needed refuge from her hated landlady duties, away from all other distractions, and a place she could escape to in the summer months. There's also some evidence that Emily may have done some land speculating herself. As well as the lot on Victoria (Laurel at that time), Emily and her sister Lizzie owned a lot on Sunset Avenue.

The year 1913, in which she built The House of All Sorts and bought the Oak Bay property, was pivotal in several respects. The economy tanked, land prices fell, unemployment skyrocketed, and a revenue-producing boarding house where she could live and paint must have seemed a solution to her financial problems.

It was also around the time that Emily stopped her travels north and restricted her painting to Sundays. That year, she borrowed $5,000 from her sister Alice to finance The House of All Sorts, and she borrowed more money from her eldest sister, Edith, to buy the Oak Bay property at what was then known as Shoal Bay.

Emily paid $900 for the land in December 1913 and built her 3.7-by-6-metre (12-by-20-foot) cottage the following year. In the 1978 book *Emily Carr: The Untold Story*, Edythe Hembroff-Schleicher says that the artist built the cottage by herself "nail by nail" at a cost of $150 and the help of "one old carpenter." But assessment cards show that the builder was Thomas Cattarall. Cattarall built Craigdarroch for the Dunsmuir family in 1890 and later worked with Samuel Maclure on the Dunsmuirs' Hatley Castle. Hardly any "old carpenter," Cattarall had a distinguished career, and by 1914 he was 70, retired, and living not far away at 800 Beach Drive.

For the next five years, Emily struggled both financially and psychologically. She hated being a landlady. "If only I could have landladied out in space it would not have seemed too hard," she writes in *The House of All Sorts*. "The weight of the house crushed me." Her book is a litany of her problem tenants and her worries about unpaid rents and broken leases.

In 1919, both her sisters Clara and Edith died. Edith left Carr House to Lizzie and the two lots to Lizzie, Alice, and Emily, the remaining three sisters. Emily sold the cottage that year for $1,200 to Ellen Hodgson Phipps, the wife of a local farmer.

The little cottage went through a series of owners and renters—mostly single women—as well as a number of alterations, including a $4,000 addition in 1983. Over the years, two demolition permits got the nod by Oak Bay Council, including one in 1989 when the owner told a reporter that the "shack" could not be incorporated into a new house. The cottage managed to survive two more years until the Davies family bought the property in 1991 and applied for a demolition permit. They tried to give the cottage to the provincial government, which runs Carr House, but officials said no thanks.

When Terri Tallentire first heard that Emily's cottage refuge was to be ripped down and discarded, she was horrified. She thought at the least it should be put into a park or made into a tea house. And, when city workers told her the cottage was coming down in three days' time, she swung into action. "I thought, oh my God, they are serious. We went into the municipality and said, 'Look, would somebody come over and look at our backyard to see if we can put it in there?'"

At the time, Terri, an English teacher, lived in a heritage house at 825 Foul Bay Road. Designed by Samuel Maclure, "Eltham" is a 557-square-metre (6,000-square-foot) house, framed by stone walls and box hedges, and set in a large garden surrounded by other stately old manors.

An artist herself, and briefly the co-owner of an art gallery in Victoria, Terri liked the connection to Maclure. Both the architect and Carr were charter members of the Island Arts and Crafts Society, though Emily's relationship with the society was an uneasy one. "They liked what they liked—would tolerate no innovations," writes Emily in *The House of All Sorts*. "My change in thought and expression had angered them into fierce indecency. They ridiculed my striving for bigness, depth."

By the time the cottage ended up in the Tallentires' backyard, the original two rooms were significantly altered. Terri removed the half-log siding to uncover board-and-batten siding, kept the original wooden shingles and interior chimney, and found windows that came close to the ones Emily would have installed. She painted them white.

The Tallentires have since moved, but Emily Carr's original cottage still sits at the back of their former property. "It's not a grand building. It's just that it has a little bit of history and it's part of her story," says Terri.

After Emily's death in 1945, Nellie McClung, her friend and fellow author, writes: "Emily Carr was a shining link with the past. She was essentially a trailbreaker, not afraid to make a new pattern with her pen or a paint brush. She wrote as she pleased and painted her world as she saw it."

NELLIE MCCLUNG (1873–1951)

1861 Ferndale Road, Gordon Head

Judith Terry knelt down beside the old coach house and started to sweep the concrete with a hand brush. A family of five deer, all as tame as pet dogs, stood by and watched her. As decades of dirt came away, the name Nellie Mc-Clung began to surface. The date was a bit harder to read, but the year 1935 appeared underneath the famous name.

When Nellie had moved to Gordon Head and started making sauerkraut and dill pickles from her garden, few of her neighbours realized how famous she was until a 1974 stamp honoured the 100th anniversary of her birth. In 1999, when Canadians were asked to nominate the top 20 Canadian heroes, Nellie came in 10th, just behind Billy Bishop and ahead of John Diefenbaker, Alexander Graham Bell, Lucy Maud Montgomery, and Joey Smallwood.

By the time Nellie "retired" to Gordon Head in 1935, she had notched up a long list of accomplishments. In 1900, when she was 27, a woman's salary was legally the property of her husband. He had control of their children, and of her. The law defined an eligible voter as "a male person, including an Indian and excluding a person of Mongolian or Chinese race." And, if that wasn't clear enough, the Election Act went on to say: "No woman, idiot, lunatic or criminal shall vote."

Nellie fought against social injustice and campaigned for women's rights, and her list of accomplishments is long and awe-inspiring. In the early days of the 20th century, Nellie and her pharmacist husband, Wes, raised five kids in rural Manitoba. By 1908, she had written the first of 16 books. That novel, *Sowing Seeds in Danny*, sold over 100,000 copies—outselling Lucy Maud Montgomery's *Anne of Green Gables*, which came out the same year—in a country where 5,000 is still considered a bestseller.

In 1916, she was instrumental in getting women the vote in Manitoba—the first province to grant this right. In 1928, she was one of five Alberta women who went to the Supreme Court of Canada to insist women be included as "persons," making them eligible to be named to the Senate. A monument to Canada's Famous Five was unveiled in Calgary in 1999 to mark the 70th anniversary of the "Persons" case. A replica also sits on Parliament Hill in Ottawa.

Judith, a retired University of Victoria English professor, and her husband, Reg, have lived in Nellie McClung's former home since 1981. They bought the house almost by accident. The house they were living in had grown too small and they were trying to decide whether to renovate or upgrade.

"The newspaper had just come out and the house was on the back cover. It just said 'Gordon House Special' and there was half an acre of land with a coach house," Judith says. "It was love at first sight. I knew I had to have it."

Nellie McClung's home was known as "Lantern Lane" after the books she wrote in her upstairs study. PHOTO CA.1960, COURTESY SAANICH ARCHIVES 1981-023-004B

Judith knew nothing of Nellie McClung at the time, except that some years before she had read *Sowing Seeds in Danny*. After they moved in, she started researching former owners and discovered that she and Nellie had a lot in common.

She found out that locals knew the house as "Lantern Lane," named after Nellie's two "Lantern Lane" books written from her upstairs study, now the Terrys' bedroom. The room looks out to the ocean and onto a gigantic monkey puzzle tree, possibly planted by John Fullerton, the original owner. Fullerton, a strawberry farmer and a former engineer on the S.S. *Beaver*, had the Craftsman house built in 1914. Neither she nor Nellie cared very much for the tree, says Judith.

Nellie named the house after a ship's lantern that her son Horace had given her and that she hung on the door of the coach house and used to light the way. The lantern is still there above the concrete path Nellie made back in 1935. Judith has painted it red several times over the years.

When Nellie and Wes first looked at the Gordon Head house in January 1935, it had been empty for several months. It was rain soaked, desolate, and smelt of wet lime. But looking past the broken windows and torn blinds, Nellie saw "the little place had the right feel. It was friendly and welcomed me in."

"Windows can be made whole, old blinds can be changed to new ones. I knew I would have bright draw curtains on the windows and the ceiling would be painted white, and I would put a light on the south wall, and my desk and filing cabinets would fit in, and I'd have a long hanging shelf for a few books above my desk—and when I looked up from my work I would see the sea!"

Retirement did not slow Nellie down. She campaigned for the Liberals in the 1935 election, became the first woman to sit on the CBC board of directors in 1936, and represented Canada in 1938 at the League of Nations in Geneva—again, the only woman to do so. She wrote another two novels, an autobiography, and dozens of columns for the *Victoria Daily Times*, all while living at Lantern Lane.

Shortly after moving in, Nellie was downstairs in the den and found John Fullerton's name on the fireplace mantel. "Then I was sure this was the house for me, for was not my grandmother one of the Fullerton girls away back in Dundee," she writes.

The name wasn't on the mantel when Judith moved in. She found the old fireplace cemented and painted over. It took her 140 hours to bring it back—she counted every hour—but by the time she finished, she had a stunning river-rock fireplace with a wooden mantelpiece.

Nellie died on September 1, 1951, and is buried in Saanich. Her gravestone reads simply "loved and remembered."

Gwen Cash, a feisty female reporter, was another writer who broke barriers. She and her husband, Bruce, moved to Victoria in 1935—the same month as the McClungs moved into their Gordon Head house.

GWEN CASH (1891–1983)

3516 Richmond Road

Stephen Winn and Sandi Miller used to go out of their way to drive past the Trend House in Victoria. The house was one of 11 display homes built in 1954 across Canada and sponsored by BC forest industries to boost retail lumber, plywood, and shingle sales.

"My wife and I are big fans of mid-century modern, and we were looking for a year and a half, and not ever thinking that we would have an opportunity to purchase the Trend House," says Stephen. "It just popped on the market and we couldn't believe our luck. We got in and purchased it, all in the space of about 48 hours."

Stephen, Sandi, and their two small children have lived in the house since October 2009.

Originally 78 square metres (835 square feet), the one-bedroom Richmond Road house was the smallest of the display homes, designed for Gwen Cash by architect John Di Castri to prove that small didn't have to mean a box.

The roof is supported by diamond-shaped trusses. Huge plate-glass windows look out onto the Sooke hills.

The sketch of Gwen Cash by Myfanwy Pavelic appeared on the cover of her 1977 memoir *Off the Record*. PHOTOGRAPH JACK CASH, COURTESY DEREK CASH

(opposite) Trend House photos by Jack Cash in 1954. COURTESY DEREK CASH

28

"Part of the excitement for us is that the architecture of that period is intended to bridge the indoors and the outdoors," Stephen says. "We are making it a family home while trying to stay true to the spirit of the house."

The social history is not lost on Stephen either.

When Gwen Cash went to work for Walter Nichol at the *Vancouver Daily Province* in 1917, she was one of the first women general reporters in the country.

Gwen met Emily Carr when she was sent to Victoria by the *Province* to interview a woman novelist boarding at The House of All Sorts on Simcoe Street. "Frankly I don't remember much about the visit except that there were all sorts of odd things strung up in the ceiling and I was fascinated and a little scared of Emily," writes Gwen in her book *Off the Record.* Gwen got to know the artist much later when she was public relations officer for the Empress Hotel and Emily lived on Beckley Street.

"The now famed painter was beginning to be talked about in Eastern Canada, but most of her fellow townsfolk still regarded her as an odd character who loved animals and Indians and painted queer landscapes," writes Gwen. "We renewed our friendship when she was living in a horrid little cottage on Beckley Street. She had a lot of rather dirty pewter on a whatnot behind the living room door and was, as she put it, making notes for her finished pictures on coarse brown paper with rather inferior oil paints because she couldn't afford anything better."

Gwen writes about how a guest at the Empress—Lady Floud, wife of the British High Commissioner—was thrilled when she found out that Gwen knew the artist. Lady Floud visited Emily at her house and bought some of her paintings.

"That evening, she and the High Commissioner were wined and dined at Government House. Full of her morning's visit to Beckley Street, Lady Floud talked enthusiastically about Emily Carr. 'But

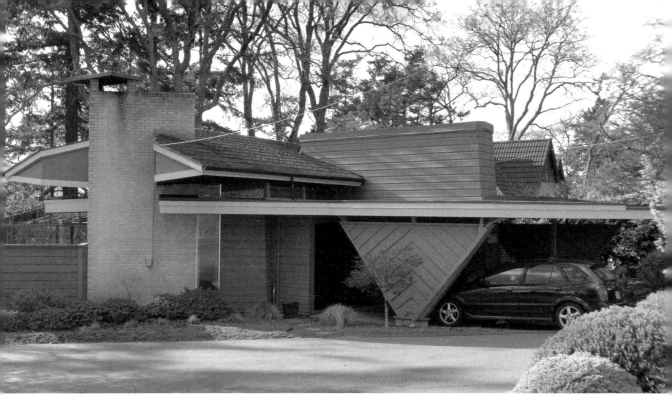

Recent photo of Trend House.
EVE LAZARUS PHOTO

who,' asked a fellow guest wonderingly, 'is Emily Carr?' 'No one knew,' said Lady Floud disgustedly."

Gwen moved around the province with her husband, Bruce, eventually settling in Victoria in January 1935. She wrote three books including *Off the Record*, in which she writes that Di Castri "designed a house that frankly took my breath away, so imaginative was it."

Gwen dubbed her house "Broom Corner" after the shrub that grew all around her and for the hybrids she planted about the place.

"Mine was the smallest of the trend houses but the most talked and written about. Conventional Victorian viewers, addicted to pseudo-Tudor or modern box construction, were puzzled and vaguely angered by its unique design. Like modern painting it was something that they couldn't understand," she writes in *Off the Record*.

Gwen went on to say she'd heard the house described as a flying saucer, a little gem, a big-little house, and a fun house.

The house was opened to the public for three months and more than 34,000 people trekked through. For months after, people continued to come from all over the world to see it.

"Who was I to say, 'you can't come in,' especially if they looked interesting, and they mostly did," writes Gwen.

When Derek Cash was a small boy he used to stay at his grandmother's Trend House and play in the broom that grew in the field across the street where houses have now taken over. Derek says he was fascinated by the outspoken and flamboyant Gwen, who would dress in ungrandmotherly bright clothes with lots of scarves, hats, and dangling jewellery.

"She wore earrings on the top of her ears instead of at the bottom just for conversation," he recalls. "She would say it was to get people talking."

She also had her three grandchildren call her "Lady."

"I don't think she really liked being thought of as a grandmother," says Derek. "We did not call her grandma. We were told to call her 'Lady.' At the time it was a name just like nanny. It wasn't until we got older that we realized it sounded funny."

After Gwen sold in 1967, the second owner added two rooms and a sun porch, and the house is now around 120 square metres (1,300 square feet). Gwen died in 1983 at 95.

Stephen says they haven't had anyone pressing the front door chimes yet, but cars slow down to look and people often snap photos of the house.

It's not surprising that the outspoken Gwen Cash, herself a woman who broke barriers, would be friends with other strong and interesting women. In "Something about Sylvia," a Province *article she wrote in 1933, Gwen interviews Sylvia Moberly Holland, the first registered woman architect in British Columbia.*

SYLVIA HOLLAND (1900–1974)

1170 Tattersall Drive, Saanich

Sylvia met her future husband, Victoria-born Frank Holland, at the Architectural Association School in London, England. Soon after graduation, they married and moved to Victoria where they designed an Arts and Crafts house in Saanich.

In 1928, two years after moving into their house, Frank died, leaving Sylvia, 28, to raise Theo, not yet two, and Boris, born a month after his father's death.

Theo Halladay says being taken seriously as a female architect was challenging at any time, but with two young children to support and on the eve of the Great Depression, it was devastating for her mother.

Sylvia rented out the Saanich house to pharmacist William Weir McGill and his wife, Gertrude, who opened a preschool there, and she moved in 1932 out to Rocky Point, Metchosin, where Frank's parents had a farm.

Gwen was definitely impressed by the younger architect. "Her hair stands up in fine hairbrush fashion over a well-shaped head. Her mouth is a bit lopsided, lifting in a humorous way over white teeth. She is tall, strong, graceful. In the evening she wears sophisticated black with long glittering earrings. But daytime most anything that comes to hand; usually riding breeches and a pull-over."

Even during the tough times of the 1930s, Sylvia managed to get two architectural commissions—the Collinson residence at 640 St. Patrick Street in Oak Bay in 1935 and the Tysoe residence on Arbutus Road in Saanich the following year. But mostly she farmed, and as Gwen writes, converted the "inconvenient pioneer farmhouse" into a liveable home shared with the two small children, and 20 dogs, cats, and horses.

(below) Sylvia and Frank Holland's wedding, 1926, Winchester, England.
COURTESY THEO HALLADAY

(left) Sylvia Holland, ca.1929.
COURTESY THEO HALLADAY

(right) The Holland's Tattersall Drive house. COURTESY SAANICH ARCHIVES

(below) Sign found in the basement of Tattersall Drive. PHOTO COURTESY THEO HALLADAY

When Boris was diagnosed with the same mastoid infection that had killed his young father, Sylvia had to move, says Theo.

"The doctor told her that Boris would not survive in the damp climate of Victoria and she would have to take him to a desert climate," says Theo. "So in 1938 we all climbed aboard the train to L.A. and my mother picked up a car that she had ordered and headed for the desert."

Sylvia put the children into boarding school and looked for work to support them.

She didn't seek work as an architect, but fell back on her art training and was hired first by Universal Studios and then by MGM as a background artist. Walt Disney hired her as one of his first women animators on productions such as *Fantasia* and *Bambi*. She worked for Disney for several years and had a stint as a Christmas card designer, then bought an acre of land in the San Fernando Valley, near Los Angeles, and designed a large two-storey house, where she set about developing the Balinese breed of cat.

Sylvia never married again. "All the single guys at Disney were courting her, but she chose to retain her independence," says Theo. "She said, 'If I had a man, what would I do with him?'"

Sylvia died in 1974, and Theo and Boris, a retired engineer, still live on the San Fernando property.

Sylvia Holland (kneeling) and Ethel Kulsar at the Disney Studios working on storyboards for *Fantasia*.
PHOTO COURTESY THEO HALLADAY

Capi Blanchet moved to Vancouver Island in 1922, four years before Sylvia Holland moved from England. Both women lost their husbands within a few years of moving and managed to survive with young children by renting out their houses. Sylvia farmed in Metchosin before starting a career in Hollywood, while Capi's book about exploring BC's coast in a boat with her five children, became a bestseller, now in its 11th printing.

MURIEL ("CAPI") WYLIE BLANCHET (1891–1961)

2457 Tryon Road, North Saanich

Capi Blanchet was found dead in 1961, slumped over her typewriter while writing a sequel to *The Curve of Time*. For a writer, that's not a bad way to go. The tragedy in Capi's case is that she died without ever having an inkling of the success her book would enjoy. There was no way for her to know that a half century into the future, her book would be republished in a 50th-anniversary edition and be a regional bestseller.

"Six months was all Capi had to enjoy and share her creation," wrote her publisher, friend, and neighbour Gray Campbell. "She never knew the far-reaching importance her work would later come to enjoy."

Born in Montreal in 1891, Muriel Liffiton married Geoffrey Blanchet when she was 18, and had five children (Elizabeth, Frances, Joan, Peter, and David). In 1922, Geoffrey left his job as head of foreign exchange at the Bank of Commerce in Toronto and the family drove out west.

L to R: (back) Joan, Aunt Gertrude, Peter. Front: Capi and David.
PHOTO COURTESY TARA BLANCHET

One day while they were driving along Curteis Point, near Sidney, the family stumbled over Clovelly, a house designed by Samuel Maclure in 1915. It had been empty for a few years, and in need of some care, but it was for sale and it came with seven acres, an oceanview on three sides, and a forest on the fourth.

The Blanchets paid $7,500 and fell in love with this rustic house, built of half logs, with lead-paned casement windows and a large stone fireplace.

Soon after moving in, the Blanchets bought the *Caprice* for $660—a 7.6-by-2-metre (25-by-6.5-foot) cedar boat. In 1927, tragedy struck when Geoffrey took out the *Caprice* one day by himself and was never seen again.

It's hard to imagine what her life would have been like. Widowed at 33 and the sole support for five children aged between two and 14, she also had to face the stigma of her husband's death—accident or suicide, it was never determined—and an economy teetering on the brink of the Depression.

"Destiny rarely follows the pattern we would choose for it and the legacy of death often shapes our lives in ways we could not imagine," she writes in *The Curve of Time*.

Two summers after Geoffrey's death, Capi, as she became known as the captain of the *Caprice*, rented out her house, packed up her five kids and Pam the Irish setter, and set off for what would be the family's annual journey around British Columbia's rugged coastline. The rent supplemented her income, and the trips would provide the basis for her book.

In the preface of *The Curve of Time*, Capi writes that her book isn't a story or a log; it was her own account of their adventures during the summer over many years when the children were "young enough and old enough to take on camping holidays."

"Time did not exist; or if it did it did not matter," she writes. "Each summer as the children grew bigger, the boat seemed to grow smaller and it became a problem how to fit everyone in."

Capi's book was first published in 1961 by Edinburgh-based Blackwood & Sons, and republished several years after her death by Gray Campbell. "She was matter-of-fact friendly, unassuming, with a no-nonsense side trying to hide a shy but rich sense of humour," he writes.

Campbell has said that *The Curve of Time* was the inspiration behind Gray's Publishing and likely responsible for dozens if not hundreds of books that would not otherwise have been published, perhaps including R. M. Patterson's *Dangerous River* in 1966, his most famous book written about his two trips into the Nahanni River Valley during the 1920s.

The Pattersons lived near the Campbells and the Blanchets. Janet Patterson married David Blanchet. "When I read *The Curve of Time* when it was first published, my governing thought was this was not the woman that I knew, because Capi comes across much more tender and sensitive in that book than she appeared to me," says Janet. "She was very matter of fact, very practical, serious-minded, and very down to earth."

Capi in the wheelhouse of the *Caprice*.
PHOTO COURTESY TARA BLANCHET

Capi was often seen wearing khaki shorts, an Indian sweater, and old sneakers while gathering firewood from the beach.

For years she refused to have a telephone because the ringing would annoy her, says Janet. Then one winter she decided to travel to Mexico, and the young couple who rented her house had a phone installed. "When she came back, there was the telephone and she found that the ringing didn't bother her at all," says Janet. "Her children had all been telling her that they wished she'd get a phone so they could get in touch with her, so now she didn't lose face with her children because she hadn't had to concede to their wishes."

Her son Peter became a geological engineer, and the two older girls, Betty and Frances, went into nursing. Betty moved to the UK and became a writer, publishing under a pseudonym. "She used to write what David very scornfully referred to as 'nursey/doctor books' where the handsome doctor always gets the beautiful nurse in the end, but she did very well and found she could earn a better living doing that than nursing."

Capi home-schooled David and Joan. Joan studied art in Vancouver, and just before she moved to New York to continue her studies, she decided to visit her mother. She bought a small dugout canoe from a First Nations reserve, says Janet, set off from Point Atkinson, and paddled across the Georgia Strait, navigating by the stars as she had been taught to do by her mother, stopping once to sleep.

"She was expecting congratulations and praise, but her mother was really annoyed with her and said, 'Just because I'm a fool, it doesn't mean my children have to be also,'" recalls Janet.

Janet and David married in 1949. "Little House," as Capi had named the Samuel Maclure–designed house that they had bought in 1922, had become unsalvageable and had to be demolished. David designed and helped his mother build a small bungalow higher up on the cliff.

"My husband told me that he learned everything that you should not do in building a house after seeing Little House," says Janet. "The old house had no foundation, it was built on boulders, and it had started to collapse."

They recycled some of the material from the original house including the leaded, diamond-paned windows. Janet, David, and their small daughter lived with Capi for one very cold winter before moving to Salt Spring Island.

"The windows let the cold air in like a sieve and the only heating facility they had was a wood-burning stove in the kitchen and a big wood-burning fireplace in the living room," says Janet. "There was a piece of curtain hung from a dowelling instead of a door."

Current owner Julie Puetter and her husband bought the second house in the early 1990s. The original leaded windows had been replaced by another owner, and

(above)
Capi on the beach by her house.

PHOTO COURTESY TARA BLANCHET

(right) L to R: Frances, Peter, Betty, David, Joan, Capi, 1931.
PHOTO COURTESY TARA BLANCHET

The living room that Capi and David built on Tryon Road. EVE LAZARUS PHOTO

the Puetters have remodelled and enlarged the house over the years, but the living room is still the same and the two bedrooms, unaltered.

"The whole inside is cedar—the ceilings, walls, everything," Julie says. "The story we were told by a neighbour was that the beams in the living room, which has a nice cathedral ceiling, were hand-hewn by Capi herself."

But while parts of both houses still exist, the *Caprice* had a less happy ending. Not long after Capi sold it for $700, the boat and the boat works where it was stored were destroyed by fire.

CHAPTER 3

Tales of the Sea

Capi Blanchet was one of very few women who featured in the dialogue of Victoria's ocean-going past, but it was literally a different story for men.

In 1905, Jack London wrote that Wolf Larsen, the powerful character in *The Sea-Wolf*, was based on Captain Alex MacLean of Victoria. MacLean, master mariner, sealer, and adventurer, was an Indiana Jones of the seas. Stories over the years accuse him of seal poaching, theft, murder, and piracy, though he was never charged with any of these crimes.

Victoria attracted many adventurous souls willing to risk their lives in search of gold, sailing BC's treacherous waters, engaged in the brutal business of seal hunting and, later, rum-running during US Prohibition.

GEORGE WASHINGTON SPROTT BALCOM (1851–1925)
127 Howe Street (ca. 1913)

Alex MacLean wasn't the only captain from Victoria to have his adventures captured in literature. George Washington Sprott Balcom (known as Sprott throughout his life) is widely believed to be the main character in Rudyard Kipling's 1898 story "The Devil and the Deep Blue Sea." Although Kipling's story was set in a south seas island and the captain had a cargo of pearls instead of seal skins, Sprott's family are convinced Kipling knew Sprott and based the story on him.

"He had an intrepid, swashbuckling reputation, just living on the edge of what was legal," says his grandson Graeme Balcom.

Born in Sheet Harbour, Nova Scotia, Sprott went to sea at 12, and by 1884 he had his master mariner's certificate. He saw huge opportunities in the seal-hunting trade in the west. He took command of a 27-metre (80-foot) schooner, sailed the boat from Halifax around Cape Horn, and arrived in Victoria in 1892, leaving his second wife, Rhoda Jane Taylor, and their three small children to make their way out alone by rail.

(opposite) Captain J.T. Walbran spent most of his life exploring and mapping the BC coastline ca.1885.
IMAGE A-02521 ROYAL BC MUSEUM, BC ARCHIVES

(below) G.W. Sprott Balcom, ca.1890. Sprott is believed to be the character in Rudyard Kipling's "The Devil and the Deep Blue Sea." PHOTO COURTESY GRAEME BALCOM

Sealing was still a lucrative industry for Victoria in the 1890s, and the crew's wages were a large source of revenue for the service and retail industries. In 1891, the *Daily Colonist* reported that there were 49 vessels engaged in sealing from Victoria, employing "678 white men and 439 Indians."

Sprott captained the vessels, which hunted seals up and down the northwest coast as far away as the Pribilof Islands, the breeding grounds for the Pacific fur seal, on the Alaskan side of the Bering Sea. In 1893, he and his crew were returning from Russia's Commander Islands, the holds of the *Marie* filled with several hundred sealskins, when the ship was seized by the *Zabiaka*. The cargo was confiscated and Sprott and his crew thrown in jail, accused of illegally harvesting seals on Russian soil.

Much later the *British Colonist* ran a story that the commander of the cruiser *Zabiaka* was "found to be insane."

Graeme says his grandfather and crew were held for over three months in a "ramshackle henhouse" in Petropavlovsk in the Kamchatka Peninsula.

"The Russians took all the seal pelts off the boat and sold them, and Sprott and his crew watched from shore as the people from Petropavlovsk rowed out into the harbour and stripped everything that was movable off the boat," says Graeme.

The story passed down in the family is that Sprott met Kipling in Victoria and told him that he and his crew escaped prison during the night, captured a rowboat from the *Marie*, and towed what was left of the schooner out into the harbour where they scuttled it so as to block the exit for their pursuers.

"Petropavlovsk is a very unusual place in that it's an almost perfectly circular harbour," Graeme says. "It's the crater of an old volcano and the entry is very narrow and very shallow, so sinking a boat there would block the harbour."

The details are a little sketchy, but according to the newspaper report, Sprott and his crew made their way to Vladivostok in a schooner, took trading steamers down the China Sea and to Japan, and finally returned to Victoria onboard the *Empress of Japan*.

The sealing industry peaked in 1894, and by 1897 there was a sharp drop in prices. Sprott saw the writing on the wall, and in 1905, he founded the Pacific Whaling Company with Captain William Grant. The company ran a fleet of vessels out of several whaling stations they invested in along the BC coast and Queen Charlotte Islands.

Balcom Inlet, near Moresby Island, is named for Sprott.

Sprott invested in steamships and real estate, and sold out of the whaling business in 1913. By this time, he and Rhoda had seven children, including Harry, born in 1880 to Sprott's first wife. Harry died in 1918 from appendicitis while hunting whales off Vancouver Island.

The family lived at 2838 Douglas Street from the early 1900s until they moved to the Howe Street address in 1922. The house stayed in the family until 1940. Graeme says the contents of the house were packed away into boxes and ended up in his father Arthur's basement, Sprott's youngest child.

In 1979, Graeme was clearing the house and sorting through the boxes. "Some of it is merely curious artifacts like an old BC Electric bill for $3 and a butcher's bill for $1.95, but some of it was seriously interesting," he says. Graeme unearthed boxes of photographs, letters, newspaper clippings, scrapbooks, and Christmas cards. His grandfather's master mariner's certificate and a painting of a still-handsome Sprott in his sixties now hang on his wall.

CAPTAIN JOHN CLAUS VOSS (CA. 1858–1922)
Oriental Hotel, 550 Yates Street (1883)

The *Tilikum* is a permanent exhibit at the Maritime Museum of BC. The 12-metre (38-foot) aboriginal dugout canoe is made of solid red cedar and was modified by Captain John Claus Voss with three masts, 21 square metres (230 square feet) of canvas, a cockpit for steering, and a 1.5-by-2.5 metre (five-by-eight foot) cabin.

The canoe looks like a flimsy little thing to take out in Victoria Harbour on a windy day, but in 1901 Voss set sail from Oak Bay, fully intending to circumnavigate the globe, accompanied by Winnipeg reporter Norman Luxton.

Voss writes about finding the canoe at an Indian village on the east coast of Vancouver Island in his memoir, *Venturesome Voyages*, and sealing the deal with a flask of "Old Rye": "The little drop of whisky, had made the old fellow feel pretty good, he presented me with a human skull, which he claimed was that of his father, who had built the canoe fifty years previously."

Voss and Luxton's adventures are covered from very different perspectives in Voss's 1913 book and Luxton's book *Tilikum: Luxton's Pacific Crossing*, published posthumously by his daughter in 1971. Luxton

(opposite/top) The Balcom family home at 127 Howe Street, ca.1920. COURTESY GRAEME BALCOM

(bottom) G.W. Sprott Balcom and Jessie on their wedding day, 1879. COURTESY GRAEME BALCOM

(below) Captain Voss sailed partway around the world in a aboriginal dugout canoe. The Tilikum in Plymouth, New Zealand, ca.1901. CITY OF VICTORIA ARCHIVES M09154

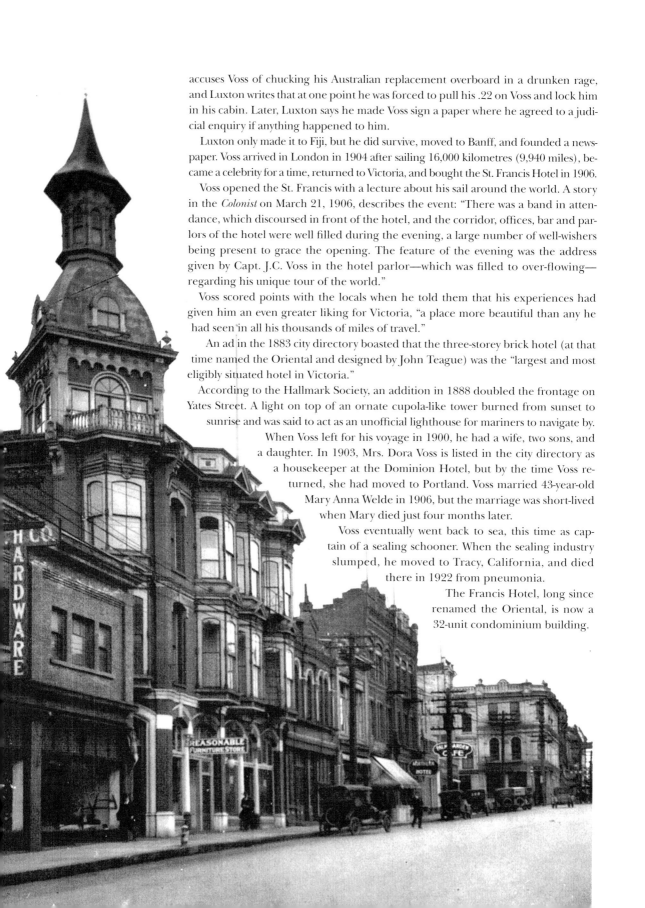

accuses Voss of chucking his Australian replacement overboard in a drunken rage, and Luxton writes that at one point he was forced to pull his .22 on Voss and lock him in his cabin. Later, Luxton says he made Voss sign a paper where he agreed to a judicial enquiry if anything happened to him.

Luxton only made it to Fiji, but he did survive, moved to Banff, and founded a newspaper. Voss arrived in London in 1904 after sailing 16,000 kilometres (9,940 miles), became a celebrity for a time, returned to Victoria, and bought the St. Francis Hotel in 1906.

Voss opened the St. Francis with a lecture about his sail around the world. A story in the *Colonist* on March 21, 1906, describes the event: "There was a band in attendance, which discoursed in front of the hotel, and the corridor, offices, bar and parlors of the hotel were well filled during the evening, a large number of well-wishers being present to grace the opening. The feature of the evening was the address given by Capt. J.C. Voss in the hotel parlor—which was filled to over-flowing—regarding his unique tour of the world."

Voss scored points with the locals when he told them that his experiences had given him an even greater liking for Victoria, "a place more beautiful than any he had seen in all his thousands of miles of travel."

An ad in the 1883 city directory boasted that the three-storey brick hotel (at that time named the Oriental and designed by John Teague) was the "largest and most eligibly situated hotel in Victoria."

According to the Hallmark Society, an addition in 1888 doubled the frontage on Yates Street. A light on top of an ornate cupola-like tower burned from sunset to sunrise and was said to act as an unofficial lighthouse for mariners to navigate by.

When Voss left for his voyage in 1900, he had a wife, two sons, and a daughter. In 1903, Mrs. Dora Voss is listed in the city directory as a housekeeper at the Dominion Hotel, but by the time Voss returned, she had moved to Portland. Voss married 43-year-old Mary Anna Welde in 1906, but the marriage was short-lived when Mary died just four months later.

Voss eventually went back to sea, this time as captain of a sealing schooner. When the sealing industry slumped, he moved to Tracy, California, and died there in 1922 from pneumonia.

The Francis Hotel, long since renamed the Oriental, is now a 32-unit condominium building.

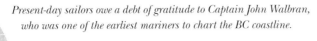

Present-day sailors owe a debt of gratitude to Captain John Walbran, who was one of the earliest mariners to chart the BC coastline.

CAPTAIN JOHN WALBRAN (1848–1913)
502 Dallas Road (ca. 1897)

Captain John Walbran sat staring out of his second-storey window, his hand resting on his neatly trimmed beard as he watched the swells of the ocean past Holland Point. In the 16 years he had sailed the BC coast, he'd explored nearly every bay and inlet, reported dangerous rocks, examined reefs, searched for missing ships, rescued stranded mariners, and serviced the lighthouses that dot the coastline.

John, Anne, and their daughters, Florence and Ethel, moved into the Dallas Road house in 1901 and lived there until shortly before Anne's death in 1907. Over the years, various owners have added a basement, bought and sold the house, and, at some point, divided it into seven units.

In 1906, and just two years retired, Walbran was writing a book that was taxing all his navigation skills and his passion for mapping and charting. That's because he wasn't just reciting place names and meanings. He was telling the coast's rich history and filling it with stories from Indians, missionaries, pioneers, sailors, and his own personal collection of research, as well as memories of a lifetime spent at sea.

Walbran found his way to Victoria in 1888 after decades spent sailing the world. He started with the Canadian Pacific Navigation Company and, after three years, signed on with the Department of Marine and Fisheries and took command of the *Quadra*.

Walbran skippered the steamship for 12 years. As magistrate, policeman, and preacher, he heard legal disputes in remote coastal settlements and enforced Fisheries regulations. On a Sunday, he could be seen dressed in his frock coat and dress sword, preaching divine service on the quarterdeck.

In a July 1906 letter to Rear Admiral A. Mostyn Field, hydrographer of the Royal Navy, Walbran writes: "The book I am writing, *Origin and History of Coast Names in BC*, has cost me no end of time and labour as it is ten years now since I first commenced gathering data."

Walbran's eccentric book, eventually called *B.C. Coast Names: Their Origin and History*, came out in 1909. Today, a first edition sells for as much as US$550. Walbran tells us that Thormanby Island gets

(opposite) Mariners once navigated by the tower on top of the St. Francis Hotel (Oriental Hotel) ca.1880s.
CITY OF VICTORIA ARCHIVES M06982

(below) The Walbran's Dallas Road home. EVE LAZARUS PHOTO

its name from the racehorse that won the 1860 English Derby. Jack Point, Nanaimo Harbour, is named for long-time resident and sailor Jack Dolholt. According to Walbran, Dolholt "had been taking his tea too strong" when he sailed to Salt Spring Island from Victoria in 1861. After his drunken first mate fell overboard, Dolholt took a lifeboat and jumped in after him, leaving the seven passengers to sail the ship into Nanaimo alone. The mate drowned and Dolholt was miffed when he eventually paddled his way to shore and the passengers refused to continue on with him.

Walbran's book is also his family history. He named Cape Anne, at Greaves Island, after his wife. His older daughter lives on at Florence Island, and Ethel Island is named after his youngest. Christopher Point in Rivers Inlet is named after Walbran's father, the mayor of Ripon, and Denison Island, is named after his son-in-law, Francis Napier Denison of the Meteorological Department of the Dominion of Canada and "a descendant of an United Empire Loyalist family." He doesn't say why he chose Walbran Island, Walbran Rock, or Walbran Point as his own namesakes.

Much of the area where Walbran worked was known as the Graveyard of the Pacific after a litany of ships including the *Coloma, Uzbekistan, Janet Cowan,* and *Valencia* sunk because of rough seas, fog, hidden rocks, and dangerous currents.

After he survived these conditions, it's a little ironic that Walbran died in 1913 at the age of 64 after a car crash. His obituary in the *Daily Colonist* called him one of the pioneer shipping men of the Pacific Coast, "a fine seaman and a very likable gentleman."

The *Quadra* had a far less dignified end. Once called "one of the finest vessels ever launched" by her officers and crew, the ship sank in the fog of Nanaimo Harbour after colliding with a CPR steamer. Salvaged and sold, the *Quadra* carried ore for the Britannia Mines until US Prohibition, then became a notorious rum-running ship. The ship was eventually seized by the US Coast Guard, with its $1-million cargo confiscated, and following years of litigation, the vessel was scrapped and sold for $1,625.

JOHNNY SCHNARR (1894–1993)
2717 Queenswood Drive

Johnny Schnarr is probably Victoria's most notorious rum-runner, or at least one of the few who talked about it. By his own admission, Schnarr made over 400 trips during the 13 years of US Prohibition (1921–1933), travelling as far down the coast as Mexico.

Schnarr was good with motors, designed boats that could outrun the Coast Guard and the hijackers, was frequently shot at, and at one time the US Coast Guard offered a $25,000 reward for the capture of his boat.

He was never caught.

"For a young fellow with a sense of adventure, getting involved in rum-running seemed like a pretty good way to make a living. I didn't get rich, but I lived well and I was good at it," he says in *Rumrunner: The Life and Times of Johnny Schnarr.* (Schnarr's niece Marion Parker taped her uncle over a period of five years and told his story through his own words.)

Schnarr gives a first-hand account of how the Coast Guard once opened fire: "I found 18 bullet holes in the hull and cabin housing, and spent a busy morning drilling them all out with a one-inch auger and banging in wooden plugs. And lucky I did. About two that afternoon a Customs officer showed up. He had a good look at the hull."

Johnny Schnarr moored his rum-runner the Kitnayakwa close to his house here at Telegraph Cove. EVE LAZARUS PHOTO

The *Daily Colonist* of September 28, 1924, also covered the story: "Watchfulness on the part of the crew of a gasboat and a fast getaway from its place of anchorage in Cadboro Bay late yesterday afternoon foiled an attempt made by Victoria customs officers to make a seizure of a rum cargo which they believe was of considerable size. The rum-runner sped out of the harbor and made off in the direction of Seattle at something over 20 miles an hour.

"To get out of the harbor the craft had to run within 30 yards of the customs boat and when she came abreast the customs men opened fire. Many of the bullets embedded themselves in the hull of the powerboat. The crew, however, kept out of sight, and gathering speed until she was hitting a pace which the customs men say was something between 20 and 30 miles an hour, she sped out of the bay and made a clean get-away."

Schnarr married Pearle Bromley in 1927, and by 1931, he had done well enough to build a home in the new Queenswood subdivision about 150 metres (500 feet) from Telegraph Cove where he could moor his boat, the *Kitnayakwa*.

Schnarr designed the house and hired a local contractor to build it for $10,200.

The *Kitnayakwa* was a shore boat, 14 metres (46 feet) long, with two 450-horse-power Liberty gas engines. It could haul 200 cases of liquor and still make over 30 knots.

In 1932 the Reifel brothers, who owned a distillery in New Westminster and Consolidated Exporters in Vancouver and Victoria, helped Schnarr finance the design and building of the *Revuocnav* (*Vancouver* spelled backward). This boat had two 860-horsepower Packard gas engines.

After Prohibition, Schnarr tallied up his savings and had $10,000 in the bank. He figured he'd spent about $75,000 on his various boats and sold the *Revuocnav* to a group that ran a lodge near Jervis Inlet for $1,500. He worked as a commercial fisherman until he was 75, then retired to Esquimalt.

Although Mabel Fortune Driscoll wasn't an adventurer or a risk taker, she did survive one of the biggest shipping disasters of the 20th century, moved to Victoria, and lived there for 47 years.

MABEL FORTUNE DRISCOLL (1889–1968)

1630 York Place, Oak Bay (completed in 1908)

Mabel Helen Fortune was 23 when she set off for a tour of Europe with her father, mother, younger brother, and two older sisters.

Charles, 19, had just graduated from high school and was planning to attend McGill University in Montreal. Alice, 24, and Ethel, 28, were shopping for bridal trousseaus for their upcoming weddings, and young Mabel had fallen in love with Harrison Driscoll, a jazz musician from Minnesota. Not surprisingly, her father disapproved of this potential son-in-law and thought an overseas trip might distract her. The two oldest children, Robert and Clara Hutton, were involved in their own lives and didn't travel with the family.

Just the year before, Mark, a wealthy real estate speculator and city councillor, had completed their home at 393 Wellington Crescent, Winnipeg, a 36-room Tudor style mansion, on the Assiniboine River. The architect, William Wallace Blair, moved to Victoria shortly after and in 1913 designed his own Tudor Revival home at 1101 Beach Drive, Oak Bay.

The Fortunes were among 50 Canadians booked on the *Titanic*. Mary Fortune, 60, and her daughters survived in Lifeboat 10. Mark, 64, and Charles were among the more than 1,500 people who died that night, their bodies never recovered.

Titanic survivor, Mabel Fortune Driscoll with Fuji. PHOTO COURTESY MARK DRISCOLL.

In April 1912, the *New York Times* carried a story with an interview with Clara's husband, who had travelled to New York with his wife and Charles Allen, Alice's fiancé. He told the reporter that Mary and her three daughters were "placed in a boat with a Chinaman, an Italian stoker, and a man dressed in woman's clothing. Of all the occupants of this lifeboat, only the stoker could row. Mrs. Fortune's daughters took turns at the oars.

"They saw the stern of the *Titanic* hoist itself in the air. A crowd could be seen struggling. Shrieks came across the water to the crew of the Fortune boat."

Mark Driscoll, Mabel's grandson and a West Vancouver realtor, says Mabel only talked to him about the disaster once when he was a teenager in the 1960s.

"She started crying and just said that it was a horrible experience, that she remembered the last time she saw her father, and that when she was out in the boat, she was crying and calling for her father and for her brother," he says. "She suffered from pretty severe depression, especially as she got older and she never wanted to talk about it."

Alice married Charles Holden Allen, a lawyer, in June 1912; Ethel married Crawford Gordon, a banker from Toronto in 1913; and probably that was pressure enough for Mabel, because she married her jazz musician in 1913. They had a son, Robert, but the marriage didn't last. Mark says he never met his grandfather, and Harrison remains a bit of a mystery, but the story passed down in the family is that after their marriage, he began to burn through the family money. "He was kiting cheques and spending my grandmother's money quite freely, and she just said enough is enough and cut him off," says Mark.

At some point, Mabel hooked up with Charlotte Fraser Armstrong, a widow with a young son from Ottawa. They moved to Victoria in 1923 and bought the Francis Rattenbury–designed house and just under three acres of garden in Oak Bay.

Rattenbury was at the pinnacle of his career when he designed York Place for Judge Peter Secord Lampman. In 1905, he writes: "I am just designing a nice house for a friend of mine recently made a judge—Lampman—he is building close to us so I am trying to do something extra nice, as I shall see it often enough."

Rattenbury lived at 1701 Beach Drive—now the Glenlyon Norfolk private school. He was the architect behind Victoria's Parliament Buildings, the Empress Hotel, several downtown buildings, and many of the mansions owned by the city's elite.

Lampman paid $6,200 for the York Place house, and he and his wife raised flowers and bred poultry.

By 1923, the year that Charlotte and Mabel became his neighbours, Rattenbury's career and his marriage to Florrie were on the skids. He had met the much-younger Alma Pakenham and was scandalizing Victoria by flaunting the affair. After he divorced Florrie in 1925, she bought a corner lot and had Samuel Maclure design the house at 1513 Prospect Place with a view of her former home.

Things did not end well for Rattenbury. He and Alma moved to England, and she fell in love with George Stoner, their 18-year-old chauffeur, who in a fit of jealousy bashed Rattenbury to death in 1935. Both Alma and George were tried for murder. Alma was acquitted, but hearing that George would hang, she stabbed herself, threw herself into a river, and drowned. Public sympathy was with young George, and his death sentence was eventually overturned.

The house on York Place was already huge, but soon after buying it, Charlotte and Mabel hired Samuel Maclure to add another wing, build a balcony off the second-floor bedroom, extend the maid's quarters, add two more bathrooms, design a large terrace with stone walls, a greenhouse, and an Olympic-sized swimming pool. In 1930, the house got another facelift when Charlotte and Mabel hired the architectural firm of James and Savage to extend the dining room and build a garage and a bathhouse.

"The home was palatial," says Mark. "It had a massive greenhouse with an aviary attached that could easily hold 150 birds."

Mark says two full-time gardeners tended the grounds, which included a formal rose garden set around a sundial, a cutting garden for fresh flowers, and a vegetable garden that produced carrots, zucchinis, peas, potatoes, and tomatoes for the kitchen.

Neither Mabel nor Charlotte's sons had much time to enjoy the house. Mark says his father, Robert, was packed off to a boarding school on Vancouver Island and sent to Switzerland to finish high school.

Robert became a mechanical engineer and moved to Montreal. Mark says that when his grandmother and Charlotte came to visit, they stayed at the Ritz Carlton. When the family went out west to visit her, Mabel put them up at the Oak Bay Beach Hotel. He remembers Charlotte joining the family for cocktails and dinner in the huge formal dining room.

"They used to have big parties and she was quite well known around Victoria," says Mark. "Once my mother sent a letter from Montreal addressed just to Mabel Driscoll, Victoria, BC, and it got to her."

It wasn't until after Charlotte's death, and his father's early retirement in 1965, that Mark and his family moved in with Mabel, Sing the Chinese cook, his bilingual budgie, and Madge, the long-time maid.

"Sing was a really good chef," recalls Mark. "He worked at Government House for many years and my grandmother stole him away from there and he worked for her until he retired."

His grandmother, says Mark, was very reserved and also very elegant. "I remember her wandering around the house in a powder blue, full-length dressing gown."

When Mark moved into York Place in the 1960s, there were two matching Cadillacs parked in the huge garage at the bottom of the property and quarters for the chauffeur.

Mabel left the property to Robert, and the house stayed in the family until Mark's mother sold it in 1989. The house is still there, but the land was subdivided and now has an additional six houses on the property. The Maclure-designed greenhouse was sent to Pender Island.

Six and a half years after the Titanic *sank to the bottom of the sea, claiming 1,500 lives, the* Princess Sophia *slammed into a BC coastal reef, and the Pacific Northwest had its own devastating tragedy, with the loss of everyone on board—men and women who formed the backbone of the north. The loss of some 350 people hit the Yukon especially hard.*

CAPTAIN LEONARD PYE LOCKE (1852—1918)
1005 Cook Street (1907)

The *Princess Sophia* pulled up her gangway, turned slowly down the channel, and steamed southward down Lynn Canal. The ship was jammed from cabin to steerage with more than 350 passengers and crew, stranding dozens who had hoped to get a last-minute passage out of Alaska before the big freeze set in. This was the stern-wheeler's final voyage of the year, and the north was emptying itself at the end of another season.

It was October 23, 1918.

At 10 p.m., Captain Leonard Pye Locke uttered the obligatory "full speed ahead." Rain lashed his face and mutton-chop whiskers as he began his inspection. Originally from Halifax, Locke, 66, had spent his life at sea. He joined the BC Coast Service in 1901 and had made the Vancouver to Skagway voyage many times before.

Quartermaster William Liggett, 25, was at the wheel, his eyes glued to the compass. First officer and pilot Jerry Shaw, 36, and second officer Frank Gosse, 28, were absorbed with the charts.

Many of the passengers knew each other. There were pioneers of the gold rush, riverboat captains, 50 women and children, and young, newly enlisted soldiers on their way to fight in the Great War. One of the most colourful passengers was Lulu Mae Eads, the same Lou that Robert Service wrote about in "The Shooting of Dan McGrew." There were 24 horses and five dogs in the hold.

Four hours out of Skagway the *Sophia* slammed into Vanderbilt Reef in Lynn Canal. The collision knocked Locke and his officers off their feet and sent passengers and off-duty crew tumbling from their berths. The jagged rocks tore into the outer hull, and, as Locke would soon discover, the *Sophia* had plowed two-thirds of her length onto the submerged mountain. Officers examined the ship's bottom, and Locke reassured the passengers that the ship was not taking on water and he was confident the ship could float free off the reef at high tide.

In the wireless room, David Robinson, the 20-year-old operator from Vancouver, sent a cable saying: "Hard and fast on reef with bottom badly damaged but not taking water. Unable to back off reef. Main steam pipe broken. Disposition of passengers normal."

Passengers stood on the deck the next day, some with suitcases in hand. Several rescue boats stood by. They could hear the piano and singing. Passengers on the deck looked calm and by 5 p.m. all had gone below.

But rather than abate, the wind increased and the snow thickened. The rescue boats left to find shelter for the night, and the passengers and the crew of the *Sophia* were left alone on the reef.

Captain Leonard Locke of the Princess Sophia, CPR photo, ca.1910. COURTESY SYD LOCKE

After almost 40 hours of pounding by gale-force winds and breakers, the *Sophia* slid backward off the rocks and went stern-first into the sea. The boilers exploded. Those passengers not trapped inside the ship suffocated in the oil from the fuel tanks.

Rescuers recovered hundreds of mostly frozen bodies from the wreck and from the shores of the Inside Passage. Lulu Mae Eads had $5,000 worth of diamonds and rubies around her neck, and John Maskell, 32, a Dawson entertainer, was found with a will and a letter tucked into his pocket.

The letter reads: "I am writing this dear girl while the boat is in grave danger. We struck a rock last night which threw many from their berths, women rushed out in their night attire, some were crying, some too weak to move, but the life boats were soon swung out in readiness, but owing to the storm would be madness to launch until there was no hope for the ship. The boat might go to pieces for the force of the waves are terrible making awful noises on the side of the boat which has quite a list to port."

The bodies returned to Vancouver on the *Princess Alice*. It was November 11, 1918—the same day the war ended.

An inquiry found that the ship was lost through "peril of the seas" and not through the fault of Captain Locke. But newspapers blamed him anyway.

Locke's grandson Syd lives in Seattle and has a poem that his grandfather wrote a year before his death. Called "Who Says Good-bye?" the poem is written in the style of Robert Service, his grandfather's favourite poet.

Syd says that Locke wrote the poem to try to cheer up a young girl travelling by herself and upset when nobody came to see her off. "The good ship sailed, / We went to sea, / But no one said "Good-bye" to me." It ends: "The Captain waved 'Good-bye' to me, / And it took all my pluck, / To stand there lonesome on the pier / And wave to him 'Good Luck.'"

Locke built a shingled Edwardian house on Cook Street in 1907. The Lockes' oldest daughter, Emily, married Douglas Blamey McConnan the following year, and they moved into a house at 629 Niagara Street. Later, Emily tried to launch a singing and acting career in Hollywood while her husband stayed in Victoria. "All the women were envious of Emily," says Syd. "She had the ability to walk into a room and have all the men around her in five seconds."

In 1913, the year the economy tanked, Locke and his wife, Emily, separated, and he sold the house to pay off mounting debts. Syd's grandmother Emily moved to 661 Beacon Street. She died in 1942 aged 89.

After the Lockes moved out of Cook Street, a local physician, Dr. J. Douglas Hunter, lived there for a time, and then for more than 20 years Wilfred and Marianne Orr ran the Victorian School of Expression, which taught singing, elocution, and drama. The house now has a heritage designation and is a commercial building for six businesses.

Syd's father, Frederick, was the youngest of Locke's five children. Born in 1891, he was with the Canadian Engineers during World War I and drowned in a tugboat accident in Seattle when Syd was 11.

"All of my ancestors have drowned as far back as anybody remembers. My mother wouldn't let me go to sea. 'It's going to end here,' she said."

After Locke died, rumours circulated that he was living with another woman and had fathered a child named Leonard. "The child was a mystery to the family for a long time. I didn't even find out about my uncle until a few years ago," says Syd.

Although Syd never met his grandfather, what upsets him most is that accounts of the shipwreck don't address the human side of the tragedy. There was Walter Gosse, for instance, a lookout and the younger brother of second officer Frank Gosse. Both brothers were at a dance. Frank made the sailing, but Walter was left behind. And there was Archibald Alexander, chief engineer from Victoria, who stayed behind because his twin daughters, Marshie and Mary, were seriously ill with Spanish flu. "How did he feel when all his friends went down?" asks Syd.

Legal battles in Canada and the US stretched on until the early 1930s. Locke's widow received $2,249.99, and his young son Leonard got $588.59. The passengers' relatives got nothing.

The first known memorial service was held October 24, 2004, at the Vancouver Maritime Museum, 86 years later. A diver had given the ship's bell to a friend in Juneau, Alaska. Later, she handed the bell to her granddaughter, Betty Mantyla. Betty held onto the bell for more than 50 years before donating it to the Maritime Museum.

Syd was at the service and so was Rosemary Irving, the great-niece of David Mearns Robinson, the ship's wire operator, as were dozens of other family members.

The bell is missing its cast iron clapper. It seems fitting not to replace it.

CHAPTER 4

Victoria's Red Light District

STELLA CARROLL

Estella Hannah ("Stella") Carroll swept down the red-carpeted staircase in a floor-length, cream lace dress, her wavy red hair tucked up inside a bonnet and her diamond rings flashing. A small white dog jogged by her side. As she descended, she called out, "Company, ladies." That was the universal signal that male customers had arrived in the parlour.

It was the first year of the 20th century and Stella had moved to Victoria from San Francisco after buying the rights to an upscale brothel. She had been visiting her friend Vera Ashton that Christmas. The same night they were celebrating the transfer of Vera's brothel, the new owner fell down the stairs and died. Stella immediately saw this accident as a great business opportunity. Victoria was enjoying unprecedented growth and prosperity. Classy brothels were in high demand. At 28, Stella was bold and brash and beautiful, and already an accomplished madam.

Stella was born in Missouri in 1872, and following the departure and subsequent death of her mother when she was 14, she was left to run the house and raise her two small brothers, Roy and Harry, and sister, Minnie. When their father moved the family to Kansas to live in a ramshackle house, she decided that her intelligence and independence could be her ticket out of poverty. With limited education, and living in a period when opportunities for working women were slim, Stella hit on the idea of running her own brothel.

When Stella arrived in Victoria, the city was a booming sealing and whaling centre near the major military base of Esquimalt and the jumping-off point for northern gold rushes. It was also well known for its red light district. Jennie Morris ran a brothel from the early 1890s to 1912 at 621 Courtney, where the Magnolia Hotel now sits. Fay Watson ran a brothel at 824 Douglas. Joseph W. Carey, a land surveyor and former mayor of Victoria, rented his building at 608 Broughton to Fay Williams, a madam. Alice Seymour owned and operated her house at 715 Broughton for 25 years across the street from what was the Union Club's second home on the corner of Douglas and Courtney. Over the years, rumours circulated that Alice's

(opposite) Stella Carroll was an astute businesswoman who owned property and operated high-class brothels in Victoria between 1900 and 1912.
PHOTO THE LINDA EVERSOLE COLLECTION, 1908

brothel had an underground passageway connecting it to the private men's club. The unsubstantiated story is that when the Union Club building was demolished in the 1950s, workers discovered the underground tunnel.

Unperturbed by the competition, Stella gave Vera $4,200 to take over the brothel and seized the opportunity to build a business that would be classier than all the others. Instead of paying her girls a wage, she had learned in San Francisco to run her brothel like a boarding house, making her money by renting out the rooms, equipping the parlour with fine furnishings and good music, and charging a premium for the food, champagne, and hard liquor she served to her customers. Stella brought her young brother Harry, then 17, with her and moved him into the brothel. Her sister, Minnie, 24, stayed in the States and had worked her way up in brothels in New Mexico. She was the madam of a going concern in Albuquerque.

(above/left #659) Jessie H, 19, ca.1912. Arrested in Stella Carroll's Herald Street brothel, Jessie gave her occupation as "book-keeper" and was deported to the US.
COURTESY PATRICK DUNAE AND THE VICTORIA POLICE HISTORICAL SOCIETY

(above/right #618) Annie G, 20, ca.1912. Listed as "actress/prostitute" in police records, Annie was deported to the US following her arrest.
COURTESY PATRICK DUNAE AND THE VICTORIA POLICE HISTORICAL SOCIETY

DUCK BUILDING

1314 Broad Street (1892)

Stella ran her brothel in the Duck Building on Broad Street, between Yates and Johnson Streets, just below Chinatown. The lower floor was the parlour and the bedrooms were upstairs.

The brick building was built to house Simeon Duck's Carriage Works and as retail space for a second-hand furniture store, the Knights of Pythias, a billiard parlour, and in 1894 the Central Presbyterian Church. Set prominently on the street, the building was surrounded by bars, other brothels, and music halls. Stella and the other madams would regularly show off their girls at the Lyceum Music Hall next door.

Stella's landlord, Simeon Duck, was a respectable business man, member of parliament, and for a short time BC's minister of finance. His son, William, was a barrister-at-law.

According to the *1906 History of BC*, Duck arrived in Victoria in 1859 and became the first wagon and carriage maker in the city. "Mr. Duck also made the first wagon to run on the Cariboo Road. This wagon was purchased by Mr. Frank J. Barnard for his express business between Yale and Cariboo," says the listing, which goes on to describe Duck as "conservative, but entirely moderate in his views."

Reporters of the period described him as a "freethinker" and wrote about the seances he held in his home on Herald Street, where he and his wife lived for more than 35 years. Apparently, this freethinking gave him a liberal attitude toward prostitution, because Duck rented out the upper two floors of his building to a series of madams. He was under no illusion about the businesses that operated there. In fact, his good standing in the community likely gave Stella a measure of protection from the police.

Aside from Simeon Duck and Joseph Carey, other owners of buildings that rented to madams included a sawmill owner, a stable keeper, a widow, a spinster, and an investment agency. These pillars of the community charged top dollar—up to 10 times the amount they could receive from renting to a family. For the madams, the high rent was just the cost of doing business.

In the street directories, madams were listed as landladies or boarding-house keepers, and the prostitutes claimed legitimate occupations such as seamstresses, florists, nurses, and musicians. Stella started with four women in 1900. In the 1901 Census, Stella, 28, is the "landlady" to Eitrym Brooks (23, "singer"), Dorothy Dean (24, "typist"), Hannah Johnson (23, "milliner"), Gladys O'Reilly (18 "actress"), and Maud Murphy (32, "dressmaker"). Several prostitutes who worked out of Stella's and Alice Seymour's brothels reported annual earnings of up to $1,800 in 1901. At a time when a typist earned $300 a year, schoolteachers around $500, and a factory worker or domestic around $200, prostitution might not have looked like a bad career choice. For some, it was just a brief stop on the way to respectability. In 1901, for instance, Ellen Holt is listed as a student living at Alice Seymour's brothel. In 1914, she married James Thomas Stonehewer, a railway conductor from Saanich.

Prostitution was tolerated as long as it operated discreetly. In a society where single men outnumbered eligible women 10 or more to one, young and attractive prostitutes often became respectable wives and mothers, their pasts deeply buried.

It was certainly a surprise to Karen Carroll Walser when she learned that the great-aunt she was named after was the infamous madam Stella Carroll.

"When I got older, I put the pieces together," she says. "But it was never talked about."

Stella never had children of her own and died in 1946, two years before Karen was born, but Karen spent a lot of her childhood with her grandfather Harry Carroll—Stella's younger brother—and his wife, Winnie, who lived in California. She remembers as a small girl playing dress-up in some of Stella's elaborate gowns that her mother had kept.

Stella rented her first brothel in Victoria from Simeon Duck, a businessman and former BC Minister of Finance.
EVE LAZARUS PHOTO

"My mother told me that Stella would buy them brand new outfits all the time. I would look at the pictures and think, 'Gosh, they had pretty clothes for not having any money,'" says Karen. "She would dress them all up and have the photographers take pictures of them."

Karen knew her great-aunt Minnie, and recently found out that the crystal punch bowl handed down to her was a feature in Minnie's bordello.

"I would go to Minnie's house in Los Angeles when we were really little. She was the more attractive sister, and I got the impression she and Stella worked together when they were younger, but later branched out."

It wasn't until years after his death that Karen learned that her grandfather had grown up in a brothel.

Harry married in 1922, settled in Long Beach, California, and raised four children—William, Jack, Mary Minnie, and Estelle. The girls he named for his sisters. Estelle was Karen's mother.

"Harry, my grandpa, never worked, but he would dress up every day in a three-piece suit and go downtown and act like he had a lot of money," she says. "He loved beautiful things and you would think he was worth a million bucks, but he wasn't. He was all show."

In the 1880s and 1890s, the red light district operated mostly around Broad and Broughton Streets, conveniently near the prestigious Driard Hotel and the Union Club. A police report issued in 1886, listed 14 brothels run by madams with a total of 38 girls. Police estimated another 100 Asian prostitutes worked out of Fisgard Street in Chinatown.

But in 1905, Simeon Duck died and things started to change for Stella.

After the Great San Francisco Earthquake in 1906, madams began to move their business up to Victoria. At the same time, churchy types gained ground. It was also the year Alfred J. Morley was elected mayor. Morley was racist, a prohibitionist, and blatantly anti-prostitution. Bawdy houses that sold booze were at the top of his hit list. Brothels were often raided, and prostitutes and madams hauled in front of the courts. Men caught on the premises were charged $50, but liquor fines were much higher.

By 1907 most of the smaller established brothels operated farther north in what was known as the "restricted area" around Herald and Chatham Streets. There was pressure for Stella to move out of the Duck Building and join them.

681 HERALD STREET
(CA. 1900)

Stella ran a highly successful operation in the Duck Building and saved enough money to invest in real estate. She bought a house on Chatham and rented it out to another madam. That venture was short-lived because the house burned down shortly afterward.

In 1907 she acquired two lots on Herald Street from a Chinese businessman named Yee Pack. One of the lots at 643 Herald had a solid four-bedroom brick home that had housed a number of respectable citizens over the years, including policeman John McDonald and Dr. Frank Hall. Stella hired an architect to renovate the house into a brothel that would incorporate her own private quarters, a parlour, a dozen small bedrooms, and more bathrooms.

Over the years, the three-storey building has been the Taj Mahal Indian restaurant, the Agra House Bed and Breakfast, and a youth hospitality-training centre.

In 1908 the Victoria Gardens Hotel and the adjacent Rockwood mansion came onto the market. Stella immediately saw an opportunity to open a top-class brothel outside of Victoria that would cater to the city's elite. It would also provide a retreat if things got too difficult on Herald Street.

Stella's Herald Street brothel was so notorious that it was renumbered from 643 to 679. It's now a respectable apartment building at 681.
EVE LAZARUS PHOTO

57

In 1908 Stella expanded her business to Rockwood—a Queen Anne mansion on the Gorge.

PHOTO FROM THE
LINDA EVERSOLE COLLECTION

ROCKWOOD, THE GORGE (1892–1923)

Rockwood was built for Joseph Loewen and designed by John Teague, a prominent Victoria architect who had his fingerprints on a number of houses in the area. Loewen founded the Victoria Phoenix Brewing Company and raised six daughters in the house. Martha, the eldest, married Francis Stillman Barnard, a Victoria city councillor in the 1880s, a member of the Union Club, and in 1914 the province's 10th Lieutenant-Governor. He was knighted in 1919 and Martha became Lady Barnard.

Loewen died in 1903 and Rockwood stayed in the family until his widow, Eva, put the house and inn up for sale. An ad in the *Victoria Daily Colonist* in June 1908 advertised both Victoria Gardens and Rockwood—called Rockland in the ad. "Hotel and acreage—large frontage on the Arm and Rockland: with 12 roomed modern dwelling and large acreage. Situated immediately opposite the Tram Company's Park. Enjoys a fine view of surrounding country. Will be sold as a whole or separately."

Perched prominently on a hill near the Gorge Bridge, Stella's Queen Anne mansion was one of the grandest in the area, a fact that would have surely rankled those respectable and well-heeled citizens of the neighbourhood. In fact, Stella's neighbours included Bagster Roads Seabrook, Victoria's first car dealer; Alexander J. McLellan, a contractor and cannery operator; John Barnsley, a gunsmith and sporting goods store proprietor; Charles Spratt, who inherited the Albion Iron Works and Victoria Machinery Depot; and Premier Richard McBride, who lived on the Gorge from 1908 until he retired from politics in 1915.

Stella furnished her brothel with antiques from Europe, expensive wallpapers, oriental carpets, and lace and velvet curtains. Fresh flowers from the garden filled silver vases. She hung a portrait of herself in the parlour.

The house was extremely private and accessed by a carriageway that wound through the surrounding forest from Gorge Road. The gardens were spectacular, with topiary and rose trellises and vines that trailed down the verandahs.

Stella's guests could arrive by road or unseen by canoe, and enter the house via a private dock and back door. Locally, Rockwood was known as "Carroll's Castle," and Stella was often seen driving her horse-drawn buggy between her two brothels. Her customer base at the Gorge ranged from prominent businessmen and politicians to visiting baseball players. Midnight raids by the Saanich police led to many arrests, and Stella was familiar with the Victoria police department and the courts.

Although Stella appeared to have little problem managing a high-class brothel, her rental properties, and the Victoria justice system, her personal life was a mess. A story in the *Colonist* on October 25, 1910, reported that Estella Carroll, a "well known member of the underworld," was shot in the leg by her companion Peter Jensen. The bullet shattered her foot so badly that her leg was amputated below the knee.

Things continued to spiral downhill. Stella's debts accumulated, the economy tanked, and she lost all her Victoria properties. Rockwood, which was registered in the names of her brother and sister, Roy and Minnie, in exchange for their financial help, burned down in 1923. The only things that remain are the two giant redwood trees that once marked the driveway.

Stella returned to California and ran a legitimate boarding house, but her lavish days were gone forever. She married her fourth husband—a boarder in her house named Martin Fabian—and seemed to live quite happily until his death 12 years later. According to Linda Eversole's book *Stella: Unrepentant Madam*, Stella died at the age of 73. She lived in a small rented cottage in California with bare floors, poor furnishings, and a menagerie of cats and rabbits.

Perhaps to make the property more marketable and to hide its past notoriety, the city in 1920 had the street number changed from 643 to 679 Herald Street. It has since changed again to 681 Herald Street.

CHRISTINA HAAS

In 1912, around the time Stella Carroll was getting out of town, Californian-born Christina Haas arrived in Victoria and set up shop. As Stella had done a dozen years before, Christina took over an established brothel.

Alice Seymour's former brothel at 715 Broughton Street (long-since demolished) gave Christina a steady clientele from the nearby Union Club and Driard Hotel. And, as Stella had done with her upscale brothel in a residential area of the Gorge, Christina set her sights outside the downtown core. Possibly because of the strengthening of the temperance movement, a toughening of the laws against prostitution, or just the desire to have a more upscale facility, Christina built her brothel in Fairfield.

Christina Haas had Thomas Hooper design a brothel on Cook Street in 1913. EVE LAZARUS PHOTO

Unidentified prostitute, ca.1912.

59 COOK STREET (1913)

According to Land Titles, Christina paid cash for the two lots in 1912 and took out a building permit in her name. Then she commissioned Thomas Hooper to design her brothel. Hooper was a highly regarded architect who at one time had the largest practice in Western Canada. His clients included David Spencer and his son Christopher of Spencer's department store. Before World War I, Hooper designed the Victoria Public Library (1904), the Hycroft mansion in Vancouver's Shaughnessy (1909–1912) a tobacco shop for E.A. Morris in Victoria (1909), the Royal Bank (now Munro's Books) (1909), the Winch Building (1912), and dozens of other public buildings and lavish private homes.

Although there is no mention of the Cook Street house in his portfolio, the signed blueprints state "Residence for Miss Haas at corner of Cook and Woodstock Streets, Victoria, BC. Thos. Hooper Architect, Royal Bank Chamber, Victoria, BC, April, 1912."

The blueprints show a house with three bedrooms, each with a separate entrance and its own bathroom.

The four-square house is built in the Classic Revival style: a central doorway with dentils in the cornice and colonnades in front. The house is now a mix of owner-occupied and rented suites, but it still features a receiving room fitted with mahogany woodwork. There are rumours that a secret door once led to a concealed wine cellar.

Neighbours tell other stories passed down over the years. The women who worked at the Cook Street brothel apparently wore business attire, and several married, raised families, and went about the rest of their respectable lives ignoring the occasional raised eyebrow and whisper.

Until 1920, Christina was listed as the owner of the property in the city directories. The brothel was then sold to John Day, a wealthy businessman, and his wife, Eliza Amelia. John Day owned the Esquimalt Hotel until it burned down in 1914. He also managed the Silver Springs Brewery and later the Phoenix Brewery. Eliza sold the house after his death in 1944.

Chief Sheppard (far left) and members of the Victoria Police Department outside City Hall on Douglas Street, ca 1890.
COURTESY VICTORIA POLICE HISTORICAL SOCIETY

Even after Day bought the Cook Street house, his tax notices were sent to the brothel at 715 Broughton Street, suggesting that he may have had an ownership stake in both brothels.

Sherri Robinson, an archivist at Esquimalt, tracked Christina to California through the 1920 Census, where she is shown living in Westport, Mendocino, with her brother, Henry Haas, and his wife, Eve. She gives her age as 58, her birthplace as California, her parents as German, and her marital status as single.

Christina's German ancestry would explain her low profile in Victoria around the years of World War I. It may also explain why Alice Seymour, who listed herself as German-born on the 1901 Census, retired from the business in 1913, and why Christina only "landladied" the brothel on Broughton Street for a year, choosing to keep her business confined to Fairfield.

CHAPTER 5

Murders in the Capital

Like all cities, Victoria has had its share of murders. Some are mysterious, some are movie-of-the-week material, and still others are just plain tragic. The murders that follow span more than a century, and all took place in Greater Victoria buildings or just outside of them. All the buildings still stand and range from family homes to a 19th-century heritage building, now a trendy shopping area.

THE KILLING OF CHARLIE KINCAID

October 11, 1898. Four hundred people crowded outside the courthouse, while the jury deliberated inside, anxious to hear the result of the week-long trial of Belle Adams, charged with the murder of her lover, Charles Kincaid (1870–1898). A little before midnight, a loud yell went up as the mob caught a glimpse of Belle, 23, and her lawyer, George E. Powell, entering the courtroom. The crowd rushed the huge doors, carrying one right off its hinges and bursting the glass in the other. As police restored order, William Fullerton, the jury foreman and a local contractor, rose to give the verdict: "Guilty of manslaughter with a strong recommendation to mercy."

June 3, 1898. Belle Adams ran back to the room she shared with Charles Kincaid on the second floor of the Empire Hotel. She was breathing hard, clearly upset, and trying to compose herself enough to confront Charlie. Her friend Fannie Lord had told her what she already suspected: that Charlie was seeing Retta Carman, that he was having a drink with her now, and that he soon planned to leave for Vancouver with her.

Charlie Brown, as they called him, was a half-black musician from Kansas City. When they met in Seattle, he was married with two little kids. Belle, blond, blue-eyed, lithe, and beautiful, was recently separated from her husband. Charlie told her stories about how well they could live in Victoria and begged her to start a new life with him there. She left her young daughter with her mother and moved to Victoria.

Soon after they arrived in January 1898, Charlie told her that he couldn't make enough money playing guitar and piano and that she needed to help earn rent and

(opposite) Belle Adams, 23, was sentenced to five years for slashing her lover's throat. Her 1898 mug shot was taken by Hannah Maynard, the official photographer for the Victoria Police Department.
IMAGE F-06721 ROYAL BC MUSEUM, BC ARCHIVES

In 1898 The Empire Hotel was the scene of Charlie Kincaid's murder.
EVE LAZARUS PHOTO

food money. The first time he set her up with another man, she was shocked, but Charlie told her it was only temporary until he could pick up better-paying gigs.

It wasn't long before they started to argue, so loudly that Mr. A.P. Briggs, the hotel's proprietor, told them that if they didn't stop they'd be evicted. Once when Belle threatened to leave him, Charlie chased her through the hotel with a knife, threatening to kill her. Another time he choked her unconscious.

It was just before 9 p.m. when she heard the key in the door. Charlie, flushed with alcohol, asked her why she wasn't out "rustling."

"I've finished with that," she told him.

Furious, Charlie turned, grabbed his open razor from the table, and swung it at her.

"Oh, Charlie, don't," she screamed. As she pushed his arm up and away from her, the razor cut his lip. He dropped it on the table and drops of his blood formed on the tablecloth next to the razor.

Belle was terrified. She grabbed the razor and slashed it across his throat and neck. Charlie clutched his throat, his clothes covered in blood, and he staggered out of the room and down the stairs moaning: "She's killed me—my god, she's killing me!"

Charlie reached the bottom of the stairs at the hotel's entrance, reeled onto the sidewalk, fell, regained his footing, staggered a few more steps, and died. Samuel Hardiman, a sealer staying in the hotel, took the blood-stained razor from Belle. Horrified residents watched as Belle flung herself onto the corpse, crying hysterically, pleading with Charlie to live, and begging his forgiveness.

"I was mad to do it," she sobbed. "I must have been, but oh, I love you so!"

She refused to move until Constable Anderson of the city force pried her off the body and placed her under arrest.

"Do what you like with me," she told Anderson.

Anderson took her to provincial jail and called for a 24-hour watch because he thought she would try to kill herself.

Kincaid's violent death made headlines the next day. At least initially, journalists had little sympathy for Belle, portraying her as a jealous woman who murdered her unfaithful lover in a fit of rage.

"Here the woman frenzied by the fear that her unrestrained and unnatural affection for a man not of her own race or color was no longer returned, half severed his head from his body with a razor," reported the *Daily Colonist.*

At the inquest the following day, Dr. R.L. Fraser told how he had found "the body of a mulatto" dead on the street. "His head was nearly half-severed from his body from a deep and extensive incised wound. This wound had severed all the blood vessels on the left side of the neck, and extended from the surface to the vertebrae. There was also an incised wound on the lower lip. The wound must have caused death within two minutes. Death was due through hemorrhage solely."

Belle sat at the end of the dock out of view of the spectators, her face buried in her handkerchief, sobbing throughout the entire proceedings.

It took the grand jury 10 minutes to indict Belle for murder.

Information about Belle is scant. She went under the names Belle, Bella, and Zella, and Adams, Ward, and Pettie. Newspapers reported that she was born in 1875, the daughter of a farmer at O'Brien's Station, Kings County, near Seattle, and married a Mr. Adams in 1895. They had a daughter, and soon after Adams moved to the Klondike. Belle met Kincaid in Seattle.

The trial was held over until October when the defence was able to locate Fred Foss, a witness who was staying at the Empire on the night of the murder and had heard Kincaid tell Belle: "I'll cut your damned head off. I told you I would do it and I will." Then Belle had screamed and cried out for him not to kill her.

The newspapers no longer depicted Belle as a jealous prostitute, but rather a young woman who killed her abusive lover in self-defence. The trial ran for a week with more people attending each day. On the last day, the courtroom overflowed into the passageways.

Public sympathy also swung toward Belle. She was convicted but sentenced to only five years in the Kingston Penitentiary.

The following December the *British Colonist* reported: "A.A. Adams, formerly the husband of Hattie Belle Adams, now serving a five years' sentence at Kingston Penitentiary for the killing of Charles Kincaid, securing a legal separation from her on the ground that she is a convict. No defence was set up, and the father was awarded the custody of the child." Belle did her time, changed her name again, and disappeared.

THE GRISLY MURDER OF AGNES BINGS

Constable R.H. Walker was walking along the track on the Indian reserve in Victoria West when he glanced down and saw a body at the foot of the railway embankment. It was a woman, completely naked, mutilated, and disembowelled. She was lying on her back with just an undershirt covering her face and some clothing scattered on the ground. He made his way down the embankment, careful not to destroy any evidence that may have survived the heavy rain of the night before.

He noted the time—8:50 a.m. on Saturday, September 30, 1899.

The body belonged to Agnes Bings (1855–1899), a hard-working mother who ran her invalid husband's business, the Plymouth Bakery at 15 Store Street (1425 Store Street today), just a few doors from the Empire Hotel where Charlie Kincaid had died the year before.

Agnes Bings was brutally murdered after walking home from the Plymouth Bakery on Store Street, where Café Mexico is today. EVE LAZARUS PHOTO

Although there was never any doubt about who killed Charlie Kincaid, the brutal murder of Agnes Bings, 44, remains unsolved.

At 64, John Bings was quite a bit older than his wife. He had been a car inspector with the E&N Railway. John and Agnes married in 1889 and had a son, Arthur, later that year.

In 1893, Agnes's brother, William Jordan, had owned the City Bakery on Store Street. He moved his business to the Vic West Steam Bakery the following year. In 1898, John took over the Plymouth Bakery and William came on as his baker. William had fallen on tough times and moved in with his sister and her husband in their Russell Street house. Agnes had run the store since John's stroke a few years before, while John stayed home and looked after their son.

In July 1899, a few months before Agnes was murdered, John Bings was convicted of "cruelly working a horse." But, "in view of extenuating circumstances" reported the *Colonist*, and most likely because of his disability, no penalty was imposed.

On the night of the murder, Agnes left work at 7:30 p.m. She had a large number of heavy parcels to carry home and asked William if he would help carry them. He told her he couldn't because he would just have to turn around and come straight back to work. He later said that Agnes would have had a small amount of cash on her, perhaps 25 or 50 cents.

In 1899 there was no Johnson Street Bridge. Agnes would have crossed the E&N Railway bridge and trestle and then followed the path along a fairly well-travelled thoroughfare by the Songhees Indian Reserve to her home at Russell's Station. It was dark, but Agnes was strong and healthy and used to the walk.

The cause of death was strangulation. According to a graphic account in the *Daily Colonist*, "there were deep furrows on both sides of her neck extending from the back of the ears and meeting over the windpipe, and in these her hair was tightly pressed showing that it had fallen in the struggle that she had made to save herself."

Agnes's long skirt, her underclothes, and stockings were gone. Her wedding ring—a plain gold band and another ring with a small stone in it—were also missing. Police searched the Inner Harbour with grappling irons, but the only items that turned up were her purse and hat. Her purse was found on the city side of the bridge by the railway station and her hat was left on the railway track near the body, probably knocked off during the struggle.

Dr. R.L. Fraser conducted the post-mortem, as he did on Charlie Kincaid the year before. At the coroner's inquest, Fraser told the court there was little blood on or around the body, and the only wounds were those around the neck where she was strangled with a rope or a strap, and at the vagina, perineum, and rectum. About 10 feet of small intestine and two feet of large intestine were lying next to the body and an ovary and her womb were still attached, but outside the body. None of the organs were missing, he said. The doctor concluded the cause of death was strangulation and that the wounding and removal of the organs was done shortly after death. The wounds, he said, were not made with a sharp knife, but with some blunt instrument such as a stick. John, William, and even poor Arthur, 10, were all called on to identify the body and give evidence at the inquest.

Police were baffled. They believed that the murderer had left Victoria in a canoe or some other kind of boat and taken Agnes's clothes and rings with them, dumped them in the harbour, or, even more bizarrely, dressed in them as a disguise and come back in to town.

At first, the police blamed the Songhees, but after finding that every "siwash" (a racist insult of the times) was accounted for, they quickly decided it was a "sexual pervert" or an "insane man." "All suspicious characters in the city have been placed under surveillance and their places of abode searched," reported the *Colonist*.

A week after the murder, the Government of British Columbia advertised a $500 reward for information leading to the arrest and conviction of the murderer. The reward attracted detectives from as far away as Scotland Yard but failed to bring out any witnesses or informants.

Police even brought in a clairvoyant, 21-year-old Agnes Harris, who lived with her widowed mother. Miss Harris went to the scene and told police that she saw a vision of the murderer wiping his hands on the dead woman's stockings and starting for town. Later, she "saw" him drop the stockings into the water and escape by boat.

Locals compared the unknown murderer to Jack the Ripper, who had killed at least five prostitutes in London a decade earlier.

According to the newspaper, police determined the "murder of Mrs. Bings to be a freak case to which the ordinary rules of professional analysis do not apply, and which will only be solvable by accident."

The murder was never solved. John Bings and William Jordan kept the Plymouth Bakery running for another two years. John lived in Victoria's Home for the Aged and Infirm until his death in 1916. Arthur Bings died in Victoria in 1953.

MURDER IN JAMES BAY

A few years after the Bests' bought their James Bay home, a young woman knocked on the door and asked if she could come and take a look inside. Her name was Neva.

(right) The Pupkowskis lived in a quiet James Bay neighbourhood in 1954.
EVE LAZARUS PHOTO

(below) *Times Colonist* accounts of the 1956 Pupkowski murder

She told them that her grandparents had lived in the cottage on Clarence Street in the 1950s, and she'd grown up believing that they were killed in a car crash.

It was only recently, she told Paul Best, that she discovered her grandfather Czeslaw (Chester) Pupkowski had died in a mental hospital for the criminally insane, more than 40 years after stabbing and bludgeoning his wife, Cecelia (1918–1956), to death in their kitchen.

"We had a bad feeling from the guy we bought the house from, but we could never put our finger on it," says Paul. "My wife had a gut feeling that this house needed to be cleaned, so we did a sagebrush burning to give it some good energy and then 10 years later we found out about the murder."

Paul says his house was built in 1906. It first appears in the street directories in 1910, owned by Philip H. Harrison, a grocer. Harrison lived there for the next decade, then a series of people—accountants, clerks, waiters, and railway workers—were residents during the 1930s and 1940s.

The Pupkowskis bought the old yellow and brown house in 1955. They had a son, eight-year-old Milo, who attended South Park Elementary School, and a boarder, 80-year-old Robina McGirr.

The Pupkowskis had met in a Nazi concentration camp in Poland and came to Canada via Germany. People saw them as a quiet and unassuming part of Victoria's Polish community. Chester, 48, was short with blond hair and glasses. He spoke little English, was a butcher by trade, but no longer worked and was often seen puttering around in the garden.

Cecelia was friendly, neighbours said, but always working. When she wasn't in the kitchen at the Empress Hotel, she cleaned houses to pay the mortgage and support the family.

68

One of Cecelia's co-workers told a reporter that she had broken down in tears several times in the days preceding her murder. The week before the murder, Chester collapsed on the street and was rushed to St. Joseph's Hospital. He was discharged after seeing a psychiatrist, who described him as being in a "nervous state."

On Saturday, March 24, 1956, Cecelia had just returned from working a split shift at the Empress Hotel. She was expected back at work at 5:30 p.m. Milo was playing at a friend's house and Robina was taking a walk in Beacon Hill Park.

At 2:45 p.m., George Warwick was standing outside his Clarence Street home when he heard a blood-curdling scream coming from the Pupkowski house. Warwick rushed inside and called police. When he came outside, he saw Chester covered in blood, half-walking, half-running toward Holland Point. Warwick followed him in his truck. He watched as Chester waded out into the freezing ocean, past three teenage boys as well as a one-armed man sawing driftwood on the beach, and started beating his head against a floating log.

Police arrived and dragged Chester from the water as he pleaded: "Shoot me, shoot me. I want to die."

At the same time, a second squad was already investigating the gory scene back at the house. Inspector Charles Webb and Detective Angus Munro found Cecelia's body sprawled on the kitchen floor, her throat slashed, and her head battered. Signs of a bloody struggle were also evident in the sitting room of the home.

Chester was taken to Royal Jubilee Hospital, sedated, and placed under police guard. At 9:30 p.m., police took him to the city jail and formally charged him with murder.

Chester never stood trial. Instead, he was sent to Essondale (now Riverview Hospital in Coquitlam) and stayed there until his death.

Milo was placed in a foster home and likely had his name changed to distance himself from the tragedy. Evidently he grew up, married, and had at least one child.

"She only came the once," says Paul Best of the Pupkowskis' granddaughter Neva. "We never saw her again."

Times Colonist, 1969

THE UNSOLVED MURDER OF WILLIAM EARL OSLAND

On Monday, February 3, 1969, William Earl Osland (1934–1969) stepped out of his Ten Mile Point home and drove to his office at Fort and Cook in downtown Victoria.

His partner reported him missing that day. His car was found parked outside his office in the wrong parking space with the keys still in the ignition and his briefcase on the front seat.

Three weeks later, his body was found in the Inner Harbour wrapped in plastic and weighted down by a 68-kilogram (150-pound) valve flange in 7 metres (23 feet) of water.

The case was never solved.

Newspapers of the time reported that Osland, who lived on Seaview Drive, had a wife, Kathleen, and two young boys. His family posted a $1,000 reward, and his mother told reporters she thought "foul play" was involved.

Osland's Partner 'Appalled'

Death Policy Cancelled

Colonist   April 19, 1969 p 1

By BILL THOMAS

Victoria businessman David Hummel, who was a partner of the late William Osland, has had $200,000 worth of accidental death insurance cancelled by Sun Alliance and London Insurance companies.

Mr. Osland's body was pulled from the Inner Harbor by divers Feb. 25. An inquest jury ruled he had been murdered.

Mr. Hummel got word of the cancellation by registered letter from George Craddock who is manager of the company's Vancouver office.

He told Mr. Hummel he was acting on direct instructions from the company's head office in Ontario and he gave no reason for the cancellation.

Premium cheques were returned at the same time, One policy was for $50,000 and another for $150,000.

"This is a thoroughly irresponsible act on the part of the insurance company and I intend to take the matter to both the federal and provincial governments at cabinet level," Mr. Hummel said. "I also intend to file a complaint with the B.C. superintendent of insurance.

"If the insurance company had taken the trouble to contact local police they would have found that I am in no danger whatsoever.

"I am appalled that there was no reason or warning given for this abrupt cancellation. To the best of my knowledge none of my other

partners have had ance cancelled.

"I believe that I did have $100,000 with the same co was personal and way connect business..."

Mr. Osland wa group of partner with Mr. Humm fied Management opment Company

Meanwhile Saanich police have reached the case and leads to follow

Mr. Osland his office. Fi pl a s tic-wrap body was foun feet of water Fort Street b

Hummel: Why me?

69

Navy divers find William Earl Osland's body in Victoria's Inner Harbour wrapped in plastic and weighted down with a valve flange.
CRIME SCENE PHOTO COURTESY VICTORIA POLICE DEPARTMENT

Osland, 35, wasn't exactly a lightweight. He was about 1.9 metres (six feet one inch) tall, weighed about 82 kilograms (180 pounds), and was an administrator of two private hospitals. Osland, lawyer David Hummel, and property developer Sigmund Marquardt were partners in Diversified Management and Development, which operated a dozen companies.

Osland was described as the "financial brains" behind these enterprises.

One of the company's recent ventures was outfitting a former US navy supply vessel for use as a floating restaurant and aquarium attraction. Newly named the SS *Tarantino*, the ship was bound for San Francisco that same week.

A witness told police that they saw Osland at 2 p.m. on the day he went missing, heading toward the ship at the foot of Fort Street—the same location where the body was eventually found. It was the last time Osland was seen alive.

Police made a cursory search of the vessel, but finding no sign of Osland, they let the ship depart for San Francisco as scheduled. Later, Saanich police called in the US Coast Guard and Immigration authorities to meet the ship on its arrival outside San Francisco Harbour. After a two-day search, they found nothing.

Lieutenant Barnaby O'Leary, who headed a 23-man homicide division in San Francisco, told a reporter: "I took nine men down to that ship myself and we searched it from *A* to *Z*. The men were in coveralls. If you're going to search a ship right, you've got to wear that kind of thing."

It's unclear what tipped police to Victoria's Inner Harbour, but 22 days after Osland went missing, navy divers found his bludgeoned body in the water.

At an inquest on February 28, pathologist Kenneth Thornton said that Osland's massive head wounds were the result of three blows by a blunt instrument and that they were of an irregular, ragged nature. He said they were "lunar-shaped" and ranged from 1.9 to 3.8 centimetres (three-quarters of an inch to an inch and a half) in length. Sometime before his death, both of Osland's wrists and his right ankle were bruised. A separate injury was also inflicted above Osland's right eye, suggesting a struggle with more than one assailant.

The pathologist told the court that Osland's body had been in the water about three weeks —the same length of time he had been missing. He also said that the absence of water in the lungs and stomach indicated that death had occurred before the body was placed in the water.

In April, two months after the discovery of Osland's body, his former partner David Hummel had $200,000 worth of accidental death insurance cancelled by Sun Alliance and London Insurance Companies. He was given no reason for the cancellation and his cheques were returned. "If the insurance company had taken the trouble to contact local police they would have found that I am in no danger whatsoever," he told the *Times Colonist*. "I believe Bill Osland did have $100,000 insurance with the same company, but it was personal and not in any way connected to our business."

Osland's murder remains unsolved.

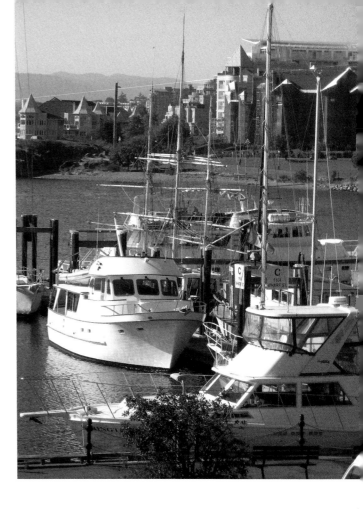

William Earl Osland's body was found at the Inner Harbour at the bottom of Fort Street in 1969. EVE LAZARUS PHOTO

THE HEAD IN THE DITCH

Doug Guyatt, 47, was cleaning up the front yard of his Colwood home one afternoon in June 1992 when he found his wife's severed head in a bag in the ditch. A neighbour watched from her window as the firefighter stood there screaming and hyperventilating, the Glad Kitchen Catcher garbage bag at his feet.

The head of Shannon Arlene Guyatt (1958–1992) was crudely hacked off at the jawline, her long, silver-grey hair shorn from her head. She'd been missing for 11 days.

The head turned a missing-person case into a murder investigation, with all eyes on the husband. And the case against him read like a TV movie-of-the-week.

The Guyatts married in March 1988 and bought the home on Cecil Blogg Drive, in the quiet, middle-class neighbourhood of Colwood two years later. By January 1992, things had deteriorated to the point where Shannon went to see a lawyer and asked for a divorce. The couple signed a separation agreement in March that gave the first $10,000 from the sale of their home to Guyatt, with the balance being divided equally between the two. The couple moved into separate bedrooms.

The motive, argued Crown Counsel Derrill Prevett, was that Doug Guyatt was bitter about the divorce and killed his wife to collect on a life insurance policy to pay off the mortgage on their house. Prevett argued that on June 17, 1992, Shannon returned home from work and was murdered by her husband. He then dumped her body, her purse, and some shopping bags, and drove her red Pontiac Firebird to a nearby street.

The problem was, without a body, police had no way to tell how she died. Dr. Kerry Pringle, a Victoria pathologist, told the court that Shannon's head had been severed from her body at the edge of the jawline with a number of sharp cuts and some blunt force. The only parts of the neck remaining were two vertebrae protruding from the base of the skull. Her head had been cut off after death, and her hair had been hacked and cropped off in a haphazard series of cuts. Although the Crown couldn't tie Guyatt directly to the murder—no smoking gun or eye-witness testimony—the circumstantial evidence was plentiful.

Shannon had told family and friends that she was afraid of her husband and that he'd raped her. A few days after Shannon went missing, Guyatt told his realtor, Richard Sims, that he couldn't afford to pay the mortgage and eat at the same time. Sims later testified that he told Guyatt that if the mortgage was insured against death, the policy wouldn't pay off for seven years for a missing person, and he advised Guyatt to explain the matter to the bank.

Police found a passport Guyatt applied for shortly after Shannon's murder, along with pamphlets on countries with no extradition agreements with Canada, an Arabic daily newspaper dated three months before her murder, and a book called *Inside Tips to Successful Job-Hunting Overseas*. They also found just under $5,000 in cash in his sock drawer. He had told his son Guy, 16, from a previous marriage, that the money was there in case police charged him for the murder of his wife.

Guyatt's other problem was that he just wasn't likeable. Married four times, he had an interesting face with a thick crop of brown hair, but had otherwise let himself go. A big paunch hung over his belt, and he confessed to hitting his wife three months before her murder. According to a *Times Colonist* article, he said that it was a clumsy attempt at reconciliation after the two stopped sleeping together. "I climbed into her bed, wrapped my arms around her, and tried to kiss her." "She became very angry and we had a loud argument." "She slapped my face and I slapped her back."

His reason for wanting to flee the country, he said, was not because he had murdered his wife, but because his step-daughter from a previous marriage had charged him with sexual assault, alleging that Guyatt sexually touched her years before in an attempt to have intercourse with her.

Guyatt also had a strong financial motive for wanting Shannon dead. "I'd rather

Shannon and Doug Guyatt were selling their Colwood home when she was murdered in 1992.
EVE LAZARUS PHOTO

kill the fucking bitch than see her get anything," he told a co-worker. "I don't know why I'm going through this. It'd be a hell of a lot cheaper just to kill her."

Patricia Harvey, a neighbour, testified that a few days after Shannon went missing, she saw Guyatt coasting his car down Cecil Blogg Drive without its headlights in the early hours of the morning. She saw the car start up at the end of the road and watched him return about 15 minutes later. She heard banging and clanging noises coming from the Guyatts' garage and a scraping noise that sounded like something being dragged.

The one thing going for Guyatt was that Shannon had resumed an old love affair with one of his married co-workers. Greg Barnes, another firefighter with the Department of National Defence, had originally lied to the police, but then admitted that he and Shannon had started seeing each other again.

He later told police that it was his "gut feeling" that "she's laying in a ditch somewhere dead."

Guyatt argued that Barnes had framed him by planting Shannon's head in his culvert.

On June 17, 1992, the last day Shannon, 34, was seen alive, she went to her job as computer systems analyst with the BC Ministry of Highways. She was wearing her long, silver hair pulled back in a pony tail and wore a blue denim dress, with a white sweater knotted around her shoulders.

She saw her lover at the small claims court when she was on her coffee break. She visited Suzy Shier on her lunch break and bought a floral blouse and silver earrings to go with a purple skirt that she brought in from home. The purchase became significant when police found a purple skirt in her wardrobe, which they said proved she did go home after work that day, and presented another problem for Guyatt, who said that she didn't. The blouse and earrings were never found.

She visited her friend Joan Wilson at Eaton's and told her that she'd be going home after work to change and to take her son Jason, 14, to baseball practice. Then she was going over to Dianne Jenkins's house, a friend who had planned to convert her basement into a suite for the two to live in.

She didn't pick up Jason and she never showed up at Jenkins's house.

Guyatt was arrested June 3, 1993, and charged with second-degree murder.

The sensational trial moved to Vancouver because of all the local publicity, took place over eight days, and involved more than 30 witnesses.

As the foreman read the guilty verdict, Guyatt, still wearing his wedding ring, squeezed his eyes shut and let his head slump forward. "Sweet dreams," a family member yelled as the overweight, sunken-eyed man was taken from the court.

In 1996 Guyatt was back in the news and in court when he was sentenced to another 15 months in jail for sexually assaulting a 13-year-old girl in the mid-1980s. "This was the final abhorrent culmination of a series of lesser but similar incidents of sexual crime," said BC Supreme Court Justice Dermod Owen-Flood.

Despite Shannon's parents putting up a $10,000 reward for information leading to the remains of her body, only her head was found. Guyatt lost an appeal in 1997, but most curious was that when he became eligible for full parole in February 2010, he chose to cancel his parole review. Guyatt also cancelled his January 2012 parole review and remains in jail.

Times Colonist story

CHAPTER 6

Ghost Stories

W hether you believe them or not, it's hard not to enjoy a good ghost story. Resident ghosts are particularly interesting, and they come in all sorts of forms. Reports abound of hearing footsteps when no one else is in the house. Some feel a presence and others see an outline of a ghost. Sometimes the ghost is mischievous and hides things from the householders. Ghosts slam doors, fiddle with electrical appliances, smoke cigars, and try to communicate with the living. Sometimes the ghost is a benign presence, and at other times, it's downright malevolent.

Some homeowners proudly boast about their ghosts, but others live in fear that ghosts will affect the resale value of their home. Not surprisingly, ghosts do not discriminate where or whom they haunt.

When it comes to Victoria's ghosts, John Adams is the expert. He's made a business out of writing about them, talking about them, and visiting them in their homes. John is also a respected author and historian, and before he retired in 2004, he worked in the Heritage Branch of the provincial government.

At first, he didn't give much thought to ghosts. In fact, he wasn't sure that he believed in them at all, but after thousands of tours and hearing hundreds of stories, he's finding the stories harder to discount.

"I'm skeptical, but I think I can now say honestly that I believe in ghosts," says John. John hasn't actually seen a ghost, but he has had experiences.

"It's usually more a feeling than anything," he says. "The ghost has not appeared in front of me or talked to me or anything like that, but the majority of people who experience ghosts don't see them, they feel them. It's a presence, it's a premonition, it's a tingle, it's a push, it's a cold feeling—something brushing past them when nothing was there."

Victoria has the distinction of being the most haunted city in British Columbia, he says, and one of the most pervasive ghosts is Emily Carr. John says that before the provincial government bought Carr House, it was used as an arts centre. A volunteer told him that every time they tried to hang a new show in the exhibit room, things would fly off the walls and move around.

(opposite) The haunted attic at the Dingle House. EVE LAZARUS PHOTO

(above) The Walker family at Heritage Lane, 1916. COURTESY BRIAN BURKE-GAFFNEY

"She knew as soon as she walked in the room that Emily was there. Even though she never saw her, she was quite sure that was Emily rearranging things in her own way," he says. "Emily has also been seen as a ghost on Douglas Street, and her presence has been seen and felt at the men's washroom at the James Bay Inn," where Emily died in 1945 when the building was owned by a religious order.

John Adams believes that one of the reasons Victoria is so haunted is because of the sheer number of ley lines—invisible lines of energy that run in straight lines under the earth and create heightened spiritual and paranormal activity.

The Fireside Grill is situated on a ley line that runs down West Saanich Road, through Wilkinson Road, toward the Four Mile House—a reputably haunted inn—to the Portage Inlet and Esquimalt Harbour.

THE GHOSTS OF THE FIRESIDE GRILL
4509 West Saanich Road (1939)
Tim Petropoulos, owner of the Fireside Grill, is a self-described skeptic when it comes to ghosts, but even he can't discount all the sightings and odd things that have happened over the years and the first-hand accounts from his staff.

"I spend so much time here at night and during the day that it does feel like there's a presence here sometimes," he says. "It feels like somebody is with you all the time. I just shrug it off, but I know some of my staff are believers."

Architect Hubert Savage designed the Tudor Revival house as an English-style tea and dance room, strategically built on a hilltop between Butchart Gardens and the new airport.

The original owners named the house the Royal Oak Inn. Its distinctive thatched roof, eyebrow dormers, and leaded windows were surrounded by a terraced rock garden, fruit orchards, Garry oaks, and Saanich farmland.

War-time rationing and gas restrictions quickly killed the business and the house was sold to John Maltwood, the retired managing director of Oxo Ltd. in England, who sought a fitting Canadian home for his wife Katharine's painting and sculptures and their large collection of antiques.

The Maltwoods renamed the house "The Thatch."

Katharine believed in the occult and wrote a book about her discovery of the Glastonbury Zodiac in 1927. This landscape Zodiac, she theorized, plays an important role in occult theories and is essentially the signs of the zodiac formed by features in the landscape such as waterways, roads, streams, walls, and pathways.

John Adams thinks that the Maltwoods intentionally bought the Saanich property because of its location.

"The house is in a really interesting location. It's on the height of land facing south with a lake behind and a ley line running right through it, so I'm sure it's not by chance that they bought there."

Katharine Maltwood's ghost is still seen visiting the minstrel's gallery at the Fireside Grill. EVE LAZARUS PHOTO

After the Maltwoods moved in, they added a two-storey studio on the north side which connected to the main building by a passageway from the minstrel's gallery. It was here that Katharine continued with her art and her writing.

Staff say the inn is haunted by Katharine's ghost and that of a little pug dog.

One of Tim Petropoulos's staff told him that he had seen Katharine a number of times as a white silhouette, dressed in a white gown with a dog by her side in her former studio.

"I've heard that she was buried on the property," he says. "I don't know if that's a rumour or not, but they did live in the house for a very long time."

Petropoulos says a number of groups have gathered on the property over the years and put crystals in the ground. "They say that there's something about the sun and the moon and the crystals that is the perfect spot for them."

Having a ghost isn't a bad thing for a restaurant, he says, especially one that's not mischievous or malevolent. But there have been incidents, he admits.

When the house was owned by the University of Victoria, caretakers would be called about alarms going off and things going missing.

"I haven't found anything missing or changed or moved, but it's a restaurant and it's being used all the time. I probably wouldn't notice if the cutlery was upside down," he says.

Katharine died in 1961 and John left the house and art to the University of Victoria in 1964. It operated as the Maltwood Museum until the university sold the property in 1980 to the District of Saanich.

The Petropoulos family bought the property and converted the house into the Fireside Grill in 2000.

Jean Kozocari was known as the White Witch of Oak Bay. Her daughter, Tara, and Robin Skelton, a Wicca witch, poet, and university professor, would accompany her on ghost hunts. They held seances, banished ghosts, and helped eject "memories."

Tara, who also has psychic abilities, has experienced unseen forces shoving a woman down the stairs and pictures jumping off bookcases. She has assisted with cleansings to get rid of a ghost who just wouldn't leave.

Some ghosts, Tara says, are just a memory where someone is repeating the same thing over and over and over again. It's like an imprint of a past event that won't leave, a bit like an echo that goes on being repeated after the original sound has been made.

These energy fields are known to cause cold patches in certain areas of a house.

MOSSY ROCKS
2875 Tudor Avenue (1912)

When Helen Stewart, her husband, and five children moved into their Ten Mile Point home, it took some getting used to. They'd moved from a tiny two-bedroom house they'd shared with a grand piano that took up the entire living room. "It looked like a postage stamp here," says Helen.

Mossy Rocks, as it's known, is a most unusual house. It was built as a party place and the original structure was just one large ballroom with a castle-sized inglenook. The Prince of Wales (Prince Edward) is rumoured to have attended one of the early balls when the Longhursts—the original owners—had the one-acre property.

Later owners, most likely Frank and Emily Taylor, added four bedrooms, three bathrooms, and a large kitchen to the original structure. Helen, an artist, print-maker and children's author, has filled the home with a printing press and books—lots and lots of books.

The once-haunted ballroom at Mossy Rocks. EVE LAZARUS PHOTO

One of Helen's friends remembers coming to a roller-skating party in the house. Another owner used the space for hockey practice. Helen still throws art shows, concerts, and various charity events in the huge room.

It has always had a reputation as a haunted house, she says.

In the early 1990s, Helen held a house wedding for the son of a good friend who had recently died. Eighty-five guests were invited. She turned the self-cleaner on in the oven that morning and couldn't open it again. An electrician came by to try to open it, but couldn't and nobody could figure out what to do. The caterers brought a large microwave oven, set it up, and watched as it exploded. They plugged a second oven into a different plug, and it blew as well.

When Helen went upstairs, the light bulb in the boy's room blew, and when she unscrewed it, it exploded in her hand.

Later, the professional wedding photographer found that all the photos she took came out dark.

After everyone left that night, Helen woke in the early hours of the morning to find that the oppressive atmosphere of the night before had gone and there was a change in the electricity in the air. The next morning, the door to the oven opened.

"Everything had totally changed," she says. "It was so strange and whatever was there had gone, but that night there was definitely something in the house."

Most strange of all is the upstairs closet. It's a long, odd-shaped room that connects two bedrooms, in which at one time slept her two adopted sons, one with Native ancestry and the other of East Indian heritage. The closet was always stuffy, it was hard to breathe in there, and her two sons refused to go in it.

In *A Gathering of Ghosts*, Skelton and Kozocari write that sometimes a ghost is the spirit of someone who has died and hasn't managed to leave the Earth. This ghost needs to be told it has to leave, and sometimes it needs help.

"This spirit demands attention and goes about getting it by disturbing the electricity in the house, switching lights on and off, ringing door bells. It may open and close doors. It may move objects from one place to another."

Helen's spirit did all these things, and refused to leave when asked. She invited a ghost hunter to perform an exorcism on her house. The woman found that there was a nice flow of energy in the ground floor, but that changed once she got near the closet.

The ghost hunter told Helen to do a cleansing.

Helen cleansed the entire area and made the bedroom dresser into an altar with flowers and special objects. The ghost hunter said a Buddhist prayer and Helen said a Christian one.

"She said if a spirit glommed onto me, I should just invite it to leave," says Helen. "I was to go over to the open window and tell it that it would feel happier outside. I was to do the same thing with a white light."

With cedar boughs they swept the ceiling, down all the walls, and then out toward the open door and windows. Afterward, they burned incense.

When Helen finished, she looked out of the window and saw a rainbow over her garden.

"I have never seen two rainbow ends so close together. I thought it meant that I was finished and whatever was there was gone," she says. "I felt this fresh air go through the closet just like somebody had opened a window."

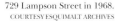

729 Lampson Street in 1968.
COURTESY ESQUIMALT ARCHIVES

Sometimes, the ghosts who stick around the longest are of people who were larger than life in their day—the ones who influenced other people's lives or were the catalyst for change. Perhaps that's the case in this haunted Esquimalt house.

THE REVEREND'S HOUSE
729 Lampson Street (1907)

Current and past residents aren't sure why Reverend Stocken won't leave, but they are convinced he's still in the house.

Sherri and Darwin Robinson bought their Esquimalt house in 1967, raised four children, and lived there until 1985.

"It didn't take me very long after we moved in to feel that there was something. I didn't know what it was, but it was something," says Sherri, adding that she never felt threatened in the house. "When we went from a hallway through to the den, we just always felt that there was something there. I would vacuum and carry on and finally I would just laugh and say, 'Leave me alone! Go do your thing—I'm busy today.'"

Sherri's daughter also mentioned that she'd felt scared to go into the room, especially at night.

The first owner of the Lampson house was Leonard Leigh, an undertaker, and his wife, Charlotte. They lived there until 1923 when they sold their house to the Stockens and their two daughters, Dora and Alice.

Not long after moving in, Sherri met Dora, who told her that her father, the Reverend Harry W.G. Stocken, an Anglican Church minister, had passed away in a chair in the house in exactly the same area that Sherri and her family felt the presence. Reverend Stocken died in 1955 aged 96.

After some investigation, Sherri found that the den was also the room where Stocken conducted marriage ceremonies. Some confetti had even been left behind. When they were renovating the basement, they found pieces of lead, and after some research, Sherri discovered that Stocken had developed a written language for the Siksika Nation (Blackfoot), in Alberta, and had printed a Bible translation in their language on a printing press in the basement. He was the minister at St. Martins-in-the-Field in Saanich, and he held services at St. Paul's Naval and Garrison Church. He was also a driving force behind the building of a permanent war memorial in what became Memorial Park in the 1920s.

"He did marvellous things and there were lots of good feelings in the house," she says.

When the Robinsons sold the house to Don and Lisa Roy in 1985, they mentioned that the house had a presence, but it wasn't until the Roy's German Shepherd exhibited some curiously alert behaviour in the room and some psychic friends came to stay that they really understood what that meant.

"Our friend saw a man with a collar, and we hadn't told her that a minister had lived in the house," says Lisa. "She also

The Reverend Harry W.G. Stocken likes to check in on his former den from time to time.
CANON HWS STOCKEN IMAGE C-09073
ROYAL BC MUSEUM, BC ARCHIVES

saw what looked like a younger woman, and we think the woman might be Dora, his daughter."

In one of those spooky coincidences, Lisa had moved to Victoria from Ontario in 1983 and was working as a nurse's aide at the Central Care Home in Victoria. One of the residents she cared for was Dora Stocken. Two years later when they bought the house, they discovered that she was the reverend's daughter.

Dora died in 1987 aged 86.

THE GHOSTS OF KILDONAN
931 Foul Bay Road, Oak Bay (1913)

Carol is a huge fan of Samuel Maclure, the architect behind hundreds of Victoria's stately Tudor and Arts and Crafts mansions for the wealthy and bungalows for the not-so-rich. So, when a suite became available at the Foul Bay Road house in 2011, Carol, a textile artist, moved from Vancouver and settled in nicely with the ghosts of three of the home's former occupants.

Carol's suite is at ground level, under the conservatory and sunroom, and faces to the east. She thinks her living area was part of the old ballroom, and her bedroom, the wealthy lawyer and stockbroker Ross Sutherland's former office. A little room is attached that once was the wine cellar. "It's like living in a museum. I love it," she says.

To understand the ghosts, you've got to know a bit about the history of the house.

Maclure designed the house for Sutherland and his wife, Martha, from Kildonan, Manitoba. The Sutherlands lost the house through bankruptcy in 1918. The house didn't become a home again until 1946 when it was bought by Count Albert de Mezey, a civil engineer originally from Hungary. The count lived here for more than 50 years before he bequeathed the property to the Abbeyfield House Society in 1998, where he lived rent-free until his death.

Kildonan sits next door to Tor Lodge, a massive chalet Maclure designed in 1907 for J.J. Shallcross. It was here that Maclure, who was also an artist and founding member of the Vancouver Island Arts and Crafts Society, attended events with other members such as Emily Carr, George Southwell, Ross Lort, and Willie Newcombe.

Ghosts are generally most active when the energy of their haunt is disturbed, particularly at the time of a renovation or a move. Carol says the ghosts were with her constantly when she first moved in, but now they come and go.

There's a female ghost who she thinks is Martha Sutherland. Carol has extensively researched the Sutherlands and found that three of their four children died before they reached 10. Only one, Victor, the first-born, survived and lived in the house.

Carol can only feel Martha's presence, but a friend who stayed overnight also saw the ghost.

"The woman appeared in clothes from the past, her hands were crossed across her chest, and she looked rather stern and disapproving," says Carol. "Martha Sutherland had an incredibly difficult run of life. She designed this house with Sam Maclure, poured her soul into the place, and then they lost it. My feeling is that it represents her creativity as well as Maclure's, and she comes back and checks it out every once in a while."

There's also a male presence who she thinks is Count de Mezey.

"He was an amazing renaissance man. He did a phenomenal amount of work with refugees. He wanted to be a doctor, but they couldn't afford the education, so he became an engineer and an inventor and made airline parts during World War II,"

she says. "He bought this house as a very wealthy man and championed plants and trees. His last passion was orchids."

Then there's the little black and white cat.

"I can see the cat, but it's not like regular sight. It's almost like 'mind sight.' You can see a cat walking across the floor toward you, and you can feel it's there," she says.

"The man who lived here before me was really uncomfortable. But if respected, the ghosts do nothing other than get too close sometimes. Then you tell them to back off," she says. "You can feel their energy come into your energy field and in me it comes across like chest constriction and sometimes nausea. Sometimes, it's a feeling around the back of my neck."

The previous resident told her that things disappeared, and Carol has certainly experienced this.

"When I first came here, I had a couple of things that were definitely moved. I knew exactly where I had left them and couldn't find them." Once when she was leaving for Vancouver she found a small piece of lapis lazuli that she'd left beside her bed at the bottom of her bag.

"They had put it in my bag. Maybe they thought I'd need it."

Former owners Martha Sutherland, Count Albert de Mezey and a black and white cat are occasional visitors at Kildonan. EVE LAZARUS PHOTO

Charlie, the murdered gardener, is believed to haunt the Dingle House's attic. EVE LAZARUS PHOTO

A house may be haunted by a ghost that has unfinished business, or as a result of a traumatic event such as a murder or a suicide. And, if there is any truth to the story of the uninvestigated murder at the Dingle House, it's not surprising that Charlie the ghost has stuck around all these years.

THE DINGLE HOUSE GHOST
137 Gorge Road East (1885)

When Barbara Brodersen was 10, she discovered a secret room in the attic of her house that was filled with books, journals of past residents, and (what she discovered years later to be) cards with the names of guests who had attended glamorous balls there in the late 1800s.

Barbara, her brother, and her parents moved into the Dingle House in 1947. The house, which sat on 12 acres, was owned by her uncle and aunt, Bruce and Gladys Passmore, who had moved out from Moose Jaw with the hopes of building a motel on the premises.

One day when Barbara climbed the little second-floor stairway to the attic, she stumbled across the house's 13th room—a space about the size of a large closet.

"I don't think people paid much attention to it because the door wasn't big enough for anybody to go in," says Barbara. "You had to go down on your hands and knees."

She remembers being in the attic and feeling a sensation of cool air whisking past her on otherwise hot summer days.

Although Barbara doesn't remember the titles, she does remember books about sailing ships and very old encyclopedias, but it was the personal journals from the Thomsons that really captured her imagination.

Charles and Matilda Thomson had the Italianate house built in 1885 for $9,000. Most likely, it was designed by John Teague, a sought-after architect at the time who lived in the area.

According to current owner Paul Chamberlain, a historical geographer who teaches at the University of Victoria, Thomson called it the Dingle House after the Gaelic, meaning "garden by the water." Chamberlain, who wrote *The Dingle House: A Century of Ghosts, Kings and Celebrities*, bought his suite in 1999 a few years after the house was shifted about 25 metres (82 feet), turned away from the water to face Gorge Road, and converted into three suites.

Paul became fascinated with Thomson. "I couldn't stop digging for more information about him," he says. "There were the detailed obituaries, an astonishing number of newspaper articles, and those faded photographs that made the past come alive for me. And still I had only scratched the surface."

Thomson, known as Gasworks because of his position at the Victoria Gas Company, was 57 when he bought the Gorge Road property. He was involved in real estate and finance, introduced pheasants to Vancouver Island, and is likely responsible for the Dingle House ghost, after hushing up the murder of one of his servants by a jealous lover around the turn of the 20th century.

As Paul tells it, Charlie the gardener was having an affair with the cook. When a young maid joined the staff, Charlie lost interest in the cook and turned his attention to the maid. When Charlie suddenly and mysteriously died, rumour had it that the jealous cook had poisoned him. Not wanting a below-the-stairs scandal, Thomson hushed up the case, and Charlie's body was quietly and quickly buried under the front verandah.

Barbara Brodersen didn't hear the ghost story until many years later when the house had turned into the Dingle House Restaurant.

"We were having dinner and somebody said that the ghost lived up in the attic. Well, they all laughed hilariously; however, I wasn't laughing as much as they were," she says.

Gasworks and Matilda lived in the house until their deaths—within 24 hours of each other—in 1916, and the house was left to relatives in England. The house changed hands several times and by 1939 was owned by Alice Cotton, who ran an elderly invalid home until the house was sold to Bruce and Gladys Passmore in 1947.

The Passmores, who also owned the Western Speedway in Langford, settled in Fairfield. Barbara, her brother, and parents lived in the Dingle House and tried to make money by taking in boarders, horses, and dogs, and selling holly and fruit from the property's two orchards while they waited until her uncle's permit to build a motel came through. When the city wouldn't give permission, he sold the Dingle House in 1950.

A few years later when the zoning did change, new owners built the Redwood Motel, and the house was a restaurant until 1989.

Paul Chamberlain has collected stories of Charlie the ghost. Past owners confessed they'd heard water running in the bathroom when no one was there. They had a poodle who was too scared to enter the attic. And they heard footsteps on the spiral staircase when they were otherwise alone. Waitresses refused to work upstairs, and lights came on and went off by themselves.

"Some feel the ghost's presence more than others," says Paul. Two old ladies from California on their first trip to the house were greeted at the door one evening by Ray Oberg, the owner at the time. "As they entered the building, they asked, 'There's a ghost here, isn't there?'"

Paul has never seen the ghost, but he has had odd things happen. "Once my answering machine came on in the middle of the night. I've had lights come on in the middle of the night. Things have disappeared. But I haven't heard banging or things of that nature," he says. "When you hear a ghost story, you start associating things that have happened with the ghost."

The attic remains unfinished.

Barbara has no idea what happened to the books and private papers, but she says they were all there when her uncle sold the house in 1950.

"I've always wondered," she says.

Sometimes when ghosts exhibit annoying behaviour—like loud banging or smoking cigars—all you have to do is politely ask them to stop.

THE CAPTAIN'S HOUSE
3808 Heritage Lane (1915)

Did Sato Fukuda's spirit travel to a former bed and breakfast in Victoria in an attempt to reunite with her husband? Sandra Gray thinks she may have.

Sato, who met Captain Robert Neill Walker when he worked for the Mitsubishi Steamship Company in Nagaskai, bore him nine children, then died from heart disease at 36 in Walker's native England, far from her family and home.

After her death in 1894, Walker moved the family back to Japan. In 1908, he left his four boys to run the family business and took his five daughters to live in Victoria.

E.E. Green designed the 595-square-metre (6,400-square-foot) California bungalow–style house. The house sits high up with views of Portage Inlet. Walker lived here until 1928 when he sold the house and grounds to Helena Von Holstein-Rathlou, the wife of a Danish count. She ran the 10-acre property as a hobby farm until 1942, a year after Walker's death at 89 at his Oak Bay home.

The property was subdivided over the years and sold to Sandra and Larry Gray in 1990. The Grays ran a bed and breakfast for 20 years, and Larry wrote *A Heritage Gem* (2010), a book about their experiences.

One of the quirks of the house is the funeral door, a door that is built into the den about 1.2 metres (four feet) above ground, but appears to go nowhere.

In the early years of the 20th century, when someone died it was common for them to "lie in state" in their home to give friends and relatives a chance to say goodbye before the burial. It was considered bad luck for the dead to be taken out the front door of the home, Larry says.

Over the years, the Grays and their guests have seen apparitions and sensed a presence. Sandra has woken to the sweet smell of cigar smoke several times. It stopped only after she sat up in bed one night and said: "Captain Walker, there's no more smoking in this home, thank you very much!"

Sandra used to hear a voice calling when she was home alone. Both she and Larry have heard people come in through the front door and go up the stairs, and when they go and look, nobody is there.

"We have one area that we call the lobby. It's a central hall, and out of the corner of my eye, I would catch a glimpse of somebody's heel or their pant leg as if they had just left the room," says Sandra.

Another time Larry was home alone working in his office in the basement when he heard the back door to the kitchen open and then close. He heard a woman's footsteps cross the oak kitchen floor and then walk down the hallway to a bedroom. When he went to look, no one was there.

Larry calls these sightings "the shadow people."

The Grays are used to serving guests their breakfast and hearing about their sightings during the night.

In 2000, Miwa, a Japanese lady in her 30s, had taken leave from her job and was spending several months at the house while she studied English. She was worried that her job wouldn't be there for her when she returned. One morning she came down to breakfast and calmly told the Grays that a woman holding a little girl's hand had visited her main-floor bedroom during the night. The woman touched her face and told her "Don't worry, everything will be all right, dear" before vanishing.

Another time, two women were staying in adjoining bedrooms and one woke during the night to see a ghost floating by the bed. The ghost was dressed in a long, white nightgown and wore her grey hair in tiny waves, as if she had just loosened it from braids. The woman thought the apparition looked Asian. When she turned on her light, the apparition disappeared.

Sandra is convinced it was Sato waiting to be reunited with her captain, now buried in Victoria's Royal Oak Cemetery. "I always felt that spiritually they belonged together," she says.

CHAPTER 7

Heritage Gardens

Close to a million people visit the Butchart Gardens every year. In fact, tourists often choose Victoria just to see this heritage garden. The 55 acres are a Disneyland for gardeners, with plants, manicured lawns, a sunken quarry, themed gardens, fountains, peacocks, and pathways.

The century-old gardens are still privately owned by descendents of Jennie and Robert Pim Butchart, and are a thriving industry that employs 50 full-time gardeners, 12 part-timers, and—at peak season—550 employees.

Butchart Gardens may be the centrepiece on Victoria's table, but the city has a plethora of public and private gardens, all well worth investigating.

Part of their appeal is the climate. Plants bloom from February to the end of October, and the mild weather allows a huge palette of plants from all over the world to flourish.

Although it doesn't draw close to the number of tourists who visit the Butchart Gardens, Hatley Park is a huge attraction near Victoria. Visitors are attracted to the staggering beauty and sheer audacity of the castle, and they stay on for the amazing gardens.

HATLEY PARK
2005 Sooke Road (1908)
The Dunsmuirs of Hatley Castle and the Butcharts shared the same architect—Samuel Maclure. They also shared the same gardener.

Isaburo Kishida, a landscape architect from Japan, designed the Gorge Tea Gardens, the Japanese garden for the Butcharts, and in 1909 the four-acre Japanese Garden for the Dunsmuirs. Kishida planted Japanese maples, umbrella pines, and ornamental cherry trees, azaleas, and pink pear rhododendrons. He designed a strolling garden that linked the garden's ornamental lakes with a series of bridges. He constructed different levels of waterways that were later interconnected with fish ladders for the trout and salmon.

"What I love is that you can hear the sounds of the water," says Joan Looy, who runs Victorian Garden Tours. "You can see how Kishida manipulated the streams

and how he placed the rocks by hand in the bottom of the streams to get the brook sound here and the rushing sound there. It's like a symphony."

Several of the original gardens still exist, and they and the house are open to the public.

The Dunsmuirs had the clout to act like Victoria's own royalty and their well-recorded history reads like a soap opera. Robert Dunsmuir, the family titan, made his money in coal and railways, and in 1890 built Craigdarroch, the family's first castle. James, heir to the family fortune, went into politics before building Hatley Castle, his own colossal pile of stone in a rural fortress surrounded by a wall of local granite that ringed more than 600 acres of old-growth forest.

The house is 60 metres (200 feet) long by 26 metres (86 feet) wide, with a 25-metre (82-foot) turret. It looks out onto the shores of a lagoon, about 10 kilometres (6 miles) of roads, and a view of the Olympic Mountains in Washington State.

Built for James, Laura, and their two sons and eight daughters, the house has a library, ballroom, 22 bedrooms, nine bathrooms, and one wing with a billiard room and smoking parlour that was once entirely off limits to women. There was accommodation for a dozen servants, an English butler, chauffeur, and crew for the family yacht.

In May 1910, the *Colonist* sent a staffer out to visit the estate. "We came upon the mansion from the rear. The effect could not have been more striking had it been carefully planned," writes the reporter. "For half an hour we had been plodding, in single file over a rough woods trail to the accompaniment of the blue grouse's hoot-

Hatley Castle is surrounded by a wall of local granite that rings more than 600 acres of old-growth forest.
PHOTO COURTESY OF SHERI TERRIS

ing, the trilling of forest wild birds, and the call of wedges of brant geese overhead … A single step took us from the midst of this into a contemplation of one of the most magnificent houses on the Pacific Coast, the new residence of the Hon. James Dunsmuir and family, recently occupied and not yet quite completed by the architect Mr. S. Maclure, and the builder, Mr. Thomas Catterall."

James filled his woods with deer to hunt, and stocked the streams with trout and salmon.

In 1912, he hired Boston landscapers Brett and Hall to design the Edwardian rose garden and a formal, walled Italian terrace garden. They planned the curving driveways and a croquet lawn, and refined the plantings around the house. Later came the orchard, vegetable gardens, conservatory, and greenhouse. Livestock barns, a dairy, smokehouse, slaughterhouse, and a village to house and feed the more than 100 Chinese gardeners and labourers dotted the grounds.

James died in 1920, Laura in 1937, and three years later the federal government paid $75,000 to establish a military college on the property. Hatley Park became the site for Royal Roads University in 1995.

The Dunsmuirs are now relegated to the history books, their money spent, their influence dissipated, and their massive homes, tourism attractions and movie props.

If the castle looks familiar, it's not surprising. Over the years, Hatley has played a starring role in the TV series *MacGyver* and *Poltergeist: The Legacy*, and the *X-Men* movies.

Richard Layritz's house on Wilkinson Road had 75 acres of sought-after shrubs, fruit trees, roses and rhododendrons, and was at one time, the largest nursery in the Pacific Northwest.
PHOTO CA.1912, COURTESY SAANICH ARCHIVES
1985-008-008A

LAYRITZ NURSERY
4354 Wilkinson Road (1889)

Dozens of the rhododendrons that bloom at Hatley Park originated in the Layritz Nursery on Wilkinson Road. The Dunsmuirs, the Butcharts, and many of Samuel Maclure's clients—including the Sutherlands at Kildonan—frequented this nursery.

Richard Layritz's house on Wilkinson still exists, but it's hidden behind a large fence, a wall of trees, and No Trespassing signs. The only evidence that this property was once 75 acres of sought-after shrubs, fruit trees, roses, and rhododendrons is a plaque on the giant sequoia that sits at the front, telling visitors that it was planted by Richard Layritz in 1889, and that his ashes and those of his wife, Dorothy, are scattered under the massive redwood—Saanich's oldest heritage tree.

Born in Germany, Layritz studied horticulture in Stuttgart, ornamental gardening in Paris, and hedging in London. He arrived in Victoria in 1888 and started buying up acreage on Wilkinson Road the following year.

He supplied tens of thousands of fruit trees to the Okanagan, provided Victoria's streets and gardens with ornamental trees, and sent roses to Yokohama, Japan. His rhododendrons—more than 300 kinds—grow all the way down the coast to California.

The annual Layritz catalogue was a highlight for gardeners and religiously read and followed by the locals. During the 1920s and 1930s, the Layritz Nursery was the largest in the Pacific Northwest. In Layritz's day, the huge barn was a packing house. There was also a carriage house, a blacksmith's cottage, and the stables near today's playing fields. His library was filled with German books, he had a piano brought from Germany, and he kept a cellar for his wine.

His motto was "Love the plants and they will grow." He would apparently refuse to sell to people who he thought wouldn't take care of them.

Before he died in 1954, Layritz donated several acres of his land to the District of Saanich, and after his death, Dorothy donated several more. The land is now called Layritz Park.

ABKHAZI GARDEN
1964 Fairfield Road (1947)

When Peggy Pemberton-Carter bought five acres of newly subdivided land on a rocky Fairfield lot in 1946, her slice of Victoria stretched all the way to Foul Bay Road. She hired landscapers to clear the land, created a meandering lawn, planted heathers, and contracted local architect John Wade to design a tiny summer house. That same year, she found that her prince, Nicholas Abkhazi, a Georgian exile, had also survived the war and was living in New York. They married and returned to Victoria.

Over the years portions of the land was sold off as the Abkhazis needed more money to support their garden. The Abkhazi Garden is now just over an acre, with natural rock, ponds filled with mallards, curvy pathways, and a series of distinctive spaces that flow together to replicate a Chinese garden. Nicholas's and Peggy's ashes rest at the base of the rock at the north end of the lawn. This magical garden is now managed by the Land Conservancy and tended by 25 dedicated volunteers.

Peggy Abkhazi, ca. 1990, once told a reporter that she moved to Victoria because she'd heard that it was a place where a person could be as eccentric as they wanted and nobody would notice.
PHOTO COURTESY UVIC ARCHIVES
1990-068-801-804

Jeff de Jong, site manager and head gardener, says the garden is often touted as one of the top hundred small gardens of the world, and a garden that you must see, but it still remains unknown to many locals.

"It always comes as a bit of a shock to me that people have lived here all their lives and never visited the garden," he says. "But I have to remember that it was a private residence and because the Abkhazis didn't want to attract attention, there's the barrier on the street and people don't see what's here in the garden."

The summer house gave Peggy and Nicholas shelter and a place to make a light meal while they planned their main residence and set about cultivating a garden out of rock and weeds.

They chose daffodils, tulips, and aubrietia for a fast show of colour and planted a hornbeam hedge for privacy. Gradually, they added heathers, hybrid brooms, blue spruces, and other conifers. They planted ferns, cyclamen, and primroses, and added mature rhododendrons and azaleas from as far away as Siberia, Burma, and the Himalayas.

The modest house that the Abkhazi's built in 1947 had the first heated floor in Victoria.
EVE LAZARUS PHOTO

The garden influenced the design of their modest house on the large rock where they had once watched the sunset. The house, designed by John Wade, is small, with vaulted ceilings, natural wood and stone, and the first heated floor in Victoria. The living room with its wall-to-wall windows looks out on Juan de Fuca Strait and the Olympic Mountains, and is now a restaurant. A gift shop is in the Abkhazis' former bedroom. The garden spills out from the house and looks over woodland filled with towering, century-old rhododendrons and native Garry oaks.

The garden gradually grew into its rocky outcroppings and Garry oaks. The Abkhazis created pathways and chose plants that would enhance the natural landscape—Japanese maples, weeping conifers, ornamental evergreens, fawn lilies, bleeding hearts, and hostas.

Jeff De Jong says Peggy had a fondness for Chinese architecture and garden design and she pictured her garden as a Chinese landscape scroll, with the Yangtze River flowing peacefully from one section to another.

"Peggy really loved the rocks because she spent a lot of her life going from place to place. They gave her a feeling of being grounded," says Jeff. "It's different from our traditional garden design style where you put the house in the middle and you

94

can basically see everything from one view. That's not the Chinese style. There's little peek-throughs, little vignettes of the garden, little vistas here and there. If you walk the garden one way, then you have to walk it the other way, and it looks totally different."

Peggy would work in her garden, her hands in the soil, her hair tied back by a diamond pin under an old scarf. Born in Shanghai, she had been adopted by a wealthy couple after the death of her English parents. She travelled through Europe and met Nicholas Abkhazi, exiled by the Bolshevik Revolution, in 1920s Paris. The pair lost contact during the war years when Peggy was sent to a Japanese internment camp in Shanghai, and Nicholas was imprisoned in Germany.

"I came to Victoria," she once told a writer, "because I heard that it was a place where one could be as eccentric as one wanted and nobody would notice."

After Nicholas died in 1987, Peggy hired Chris Ball, a third-generation gardener to care for the garden. One day he came across an old photo of his father, aged 18, working in the Abkhazis' garden. When Peggy died in 1994, she left some jewellery and antiques to her housekeeper and a chunk of the property and her dog Shamus to Chris and Pam Ball. The Balls managed the property for a couple more years, but they couldn't afford the more than $30,000 a year in up-keep. They sold the land to developers for a million dollars.

Before plans went ahead to bulldoze the garden for townhouses in 2000, The Land Conservancy of BC stepped in with a slew of public donations and purchased the gardens for $1.375 million.

"It was always Peggy's wish that the garden be kept for at least one more generation to see, and now that's going to come true for her," says Jeff.

KILDONAN
931 Foul Bay Road (1913)
Before Paul Turmel retired, he was a horticulturalist at Butchart Gardens. Now he's a resident and one of the dozen volunteer gardeners at Kildonan, an Arts and Crafts mansion with a splash of Tudor Revival in Oak Bay.

Ross Sutherland, a wealthy lawyer and stockbroker from Manitoba, paid Samuel Maclure $30,000 to design his 1,000-square-metre (10,765-square-foot) house. Since 1998, it has housed nine seniors.

Maclure had a knack for designing massive houses that blended into the landscape,

Retired horticulturalist Paul Turmel now lives and gardens at Kildonan.
EVE LAZARUS PHOTO

and he went to great lengths to avoid messing with the natural terrain. Kildonan may be one of his finest examples. The house sits high on an escarpment and is approached by a long curving drive, but it's almost invisible from Foul Bay Road. He packed the interior with Australian eucalyptus and gumwoods from Africa, and for the outside, he hired six Scottish stonemasons from Hatley Castle to quarry the granite from the land next door and shape it into the interesting honeycomb pattern on the main floor.

"Maclure came in and set the house gently on the property," says Paul. "He was careful to position the house in such a way as to respect the land."

The quarry became a rock and alpine garden, and Maclure designed a series of terraced rockeries and a huge granite grotto at the back of the house. The original five-acre property stretched out to the west and incorporated a stone carriage house, designed by Maclure and built for $1,500 in 1913. The stone carriage house is now privately owned at 2088 Falkland Road and sits behind the property's original stone pillar gate posts.

In the five short years the Sutherlands lived at Kildonan, they installed extensive rock gardens, tennis courts, croquet, a fruit orchard, and stables. By World War II, the house had become a women's barracks for the Canadian Air Force, with tents in the garden for the lower ranks. The house didn't become a home again until Count Albert de Mezey spent $42,000 on the property in 1946 for himself, his mother, and his sister, and brought some glamour back to the old place. When the count's health began to fail, he bequeathed his home and garden to the Abbeyfield House Society.

The servants and sports facilities are long gone and the property has shrunk to one acre, but remnants of its former glory are everywhere.

De Mezey was a fanatical gardener who loved orchids and rhododendrons. He shipped his rhodies worldwide, shared them with friends, and named one after his friend and fellow gardener Peggy Abkhazi. In fact, several of the rhodies at the Abkhazi Gardens originated as cuttings from this property.

Pink and red large-leaf rhododendrons flower in succession from January to July, and they are surrounded by fragrant azaleas in yellow, red, and orange. There's a fig tree at the back of the house planted in the 1950s, Himalayan and Moroccan cedars, and lodgepole pines, and the property is dotted with huge, gnarly Garry oaks, including one fabulous reclining tree that snakes along beside the grotto and runs parallel to the ground. According to a history of Oak Bay, Indian tribes called these trees "Treaty Oaks." During a ceremony, the signing parties would bend over the oak and place a stone on the trunk to hold it in place. If the tree continued to grow from this bent position, the treaty was upheld.

It's always a challenge, says Paul, to find things that the deer won't eat, and to find plants that grow in harmony together.

"It's a historical, woodland garden that's evolved in its own natural way," he says. "We bring fine gardening principles to this wilderness."

JONES FARM
599 Island Road, South Oak Bay (1909)
The Vancouver Art Gallery has a 1930s painting by Emily Carr called *Mrs. Jones' Farm*. The oil has the artist's swirling brushstrokes throughout the trees and the field, tree stumps in the foreground, and a red farmhouse and barn nestled in front of a wall of forest. The painting is of Glengarry, the Metchosin farm purchased in 1906 by Dr. Oswald Jones and his wife, Kathleen.

Amazingly, the farm is still in the family, home since 1965 to the Jones's granddaughter Gretta and her husband, Douglas. Gretta grew up on the Jones's other property in Lillooet, and lived with her grandmother on Island Road while she attended school at St. Margaret's.

Gretta's aunts took painting lessons from Emily, and their mother, Mrs. Jones, was a benefactor of the artist. Gretta says that as a very young girl, she would ride her bike around to The House of All Sorts and take money to Emily. "I didn't like Woo at all," she says. "I didn't like the monkey."

Dr. Oswald Jones
COURTESY OF GRETTA AND DOUGLAS RUTH

Welsh-born Dr. Jones came to Canada in 1891 as a ship's surgeon on the HMS *Warspite.* He had Samuel Maclure design the building for his medical practice in the now-defunct Jones Building on Fort Street. He rapidly notched up a reputation as Western Canada's leading surgeon, with interests in mining and farming.

Dr. Jones bought 38 acres in South Oak Bay for his home and commissioned Francis Rattenbury to design a 725-square-metre (7,800-square-foot) stone house built with split granite quarried on the property and a roof with slate from Deserted Bay at Jervis Inlet. The interior, designed by Maclure, included a library, conservatory, servants' quarters, and Australian mahogany floors.

When Dr. Jones died from the Spanish Flu in 1918, his obituary read "Brilliant surgeon claimed by death," with the subtitle "none will miss him more than returned soldiers," whom he treated for free. Patients came to him from as far away as Alaska, Montreal, and San Francisco, and his three-page-long obituary included tributes from leading citizens of the time.

The Jones Residence on Island Road in 1912.
COURTESY OF GRETTA AND DOUGLAS RUTH

Mrs. Jones was an ardent gardener, and a friend of Mrs. Butchart and Mrs. Dunsmuir. She grew rose geraniums in the large greenhouse and kept the property in its natural state—now a heritage tree area full of blue atlas, Deodar cedars, cypress, spruce, and Garry oaks. After Dr. Jones died, she travelled to England and France to study production techniques to manufacture perfume, soap, and sachets from lavender. She became known as the lavender lady, and for a few weeks every year, five acres below the farmhouse in Metchosin were coloured purple.

Mrs. Jones died in 1964, and the house on Island Road stayed in the family until their daughter sold in 1985.

When the property was subdivided and several houses added, more than 20 heritage trees were retained. The developers also kept the original stone gates and the fence still circles the property.

The house and the remaining land—now .64 acre went up for sale in late 2011. The asking price was just under $3 million. The garden is still spectacular with a gentle winding path that leads to Anderson Hill Park, a Garry oaks ecosystem.

The red house that Emily painted is still there at Glengarry, and it's still red. Designed by Frank Owen in 1909, the house was built for the farm manager and sits just above a five-thousand-year-old aboriginal midden.

THE MUNRO/SABISTON GARDEN
1648 Rockland Avenue (1894)

Carole Sabiston and Jim Munro have a photograph hanging on their wall of three little girls in their garden. It's taken in 1904 and shows the girls dressed in white with matching ribbons taming long, curly hair. The girls are Brenda (13), Sheila (11), and Thelma (8), and they are pictured sitting in front of the rockery garden and a huge planting of Shasta daisies which still exists today.

The girls are the daughters of Alan Dumbleton, a barrister from South Africa, and his wife, Mabel, the original owners of the house, which they received as a gift from Alan's parents who lived at nearby Rocklands.

In 1912 Brenda married Clement Hungerford Pollen in a society wedding at Rocklands. The wedding was covered in a full-page story by the *Times Colonist*. The newspaper listed the names of every guest and their gifts, which ranged from sister Sheila's embroidered pin cushion, to a Chinese gong and a silver teapot stand from Mr. and Mrs. Edgar Dewdney. Dewdney served as the Lieutenant-Governor of BC between 1892 and 1897. "The bride," wrote the reporter, "looked very charming in a gown of cream satin paneled with silver embroidery." She wore a veil of old *point de gaze* and carried a sheaf of Madonna lilies. The mother of the bride wore an elegant-sounding "French gray striped Eolian, with a beautifully fichu of Honiton lace" and carried a bouquet of pink roses.

Brenda and Clement moved to England in 1926, and after Clement's death 10 years later, Brenda moved to a house in Fleet with their two children, Hugh and Cynthia. A few years ago, Cynthia's son, Mark Marshall and his wife, Susie, were cleaning out the attic of the house when they came across some trunks. "The trunks in the attic were filled with family stuff and of course the history of Clement's time in BC, which became the reason why we came over in 2007 to follow the trail," says Mark.

The trail led to his grandmother's house on Rockland, and to Jim Munro and Carole Sabiston.

Mark says his grandfather Clement was either a friend or an associate of Theodore Roosevelt. "I have a letter from Roosevelt to Clement in 1915, at the time when Clement was recruiting for the Kootenay Regiment. When the regiment returned from France, he was the senior surviving officer and presided at the opening ceremonies of war memorials in BC. Clement was also a mining engineer and president of the Kootenay Railway."

When Jim Munro bought the house in 1966, the garden was set in half an acre and still framed by the original stone wall. Stone turrets sat on either side of the circular driveway, which once accommodated a horse and carriage. There was an ivy-covered gazebo, a pond, and remnants of a once-spectacular garden filled with arbutus and walnut trees, hollies, Garry oaks, laburnum trees, and a hundred-year-old purple lilac.

Carole Sabiston looking at a 100-year-old purple lilac in the garden of her Rockland Avenue house.
EVE LAZARUS PHOTO

"Most of the garden was covered in invasive English ivy, so the wilderness had taken over," says Carole.

A few years ago, Carole inherited a small legacy from her mother and engaged Victoria garden designer Lily Maxwell. Together, they restored and planned the garden.

Carole created the Philosopher's Walk for Jim, owner of Munro's Books. The walk includes a bust of Voltaire. A large bush that once blocked the view from the kitchen was removed and the area was turned into the Secret Garden, a space framed by perennial borders of blues, purples, mauves, and yellows. The Terrace Garden sprang up at the side of the house, and a shade garden came to life with purple azaleas and a Japanese maple. In memory of her mother, Carole planted a pale lavender rose.

The garden already had five ancient Garry oaks, a Japanese plum, and a mixture of shrubs, and they added a dogwood, a japonica, and an assortment of plant textures through ferns, hostas, ornamental grasses, and black-stem bamboo.

When Lily worked on Carole's garden, she helped to extend and add natural stone pathways in the lawn that matched the original path. "It's always about creating a garden that suits the house, the site, and the client," she says.

Jim Munro and Carole Sabiston's Rockland Avenue house.
EVE LAZARUS PHOTO

LILY MAXWELL'S GARDEN
260 King George Terrace (ca. 1935)

Lily Maxwell says a garden should always reflect the people who live there.

"When you look at your garden, it should transform you in some way," she says. "It should lower your blood pressure, it should make you feel more tranquil, and it should speak to you."

Lily is a professional garden designer who likes to use plant combinations to provide blocks of colour and texture.

"Because I'm a designer, I work hard at arranging, so it's not just a collection of plants, it's something that looks good as a whole," she says. "I like to work with colour blocks. I like limited colour palettes. I don't want a riot of colour, and I don't want the whole garden to look the same."

In Lily's garden is a side garden that is blue and white in the summer, filled with agapanthus from South Africa, white casablancas, hydrangeas, and Stargazer lilies. In August, a section of her back garden will sprout a red border of roses, dahlias, and other perennials. Another section is filled with Golden Hawk, pale yellow clematis, and apricot- and chartreuse-coloured flowers.

Lily Maxwell says that when you look at your garden it should transform you in some way. Her own garden surrounds a 1930s Oak Bay house.

Lily Maxwell says that a garden should always reflect the people who live there.
EVE LAZARUS PHOTO

The succession of blooms starts in February and goes through to the end of October.

Lily's garden has been a work in progress since 1988, when she, a full-time elementary teacher with three children, moved into the house. Its half acre of land was mostly lawn, hedge, and self-seeded fruit trees.

"I just made it my goal to develop a section of the garden every year, and learn how to do it properly," she says.

She started by taking out over 30 trees and began to create and shape the beds. A section that catches the early morning sun is now the woodland garden.

In 1999, Lily's garden won a national competition through *Canadian Gardening* magazine for best garden. Her prize was a 16-day cruise on the Danube, and the win gave her the confidence to go beyond home gardening. In 2005, she dove right into full-time garden design.

The garden surrounds a 1930s South Oak Bay house and slopes down gently to the road. The lawn is broken up by borders and a series of distinctive garden spaces. Each of the mixed borders has its own distinct character, including woodland, Mediterranean, and a rockery.

In the back, one-metre-wide (3-feet-wide) gravel pathways wind through the garden beds, a variety of rare plants from China and South America, and a 12-metre (40-foot) eucalyptus tree from Australia. A formal, intricate knot garden spills out from the back patio, and to the side, a giant plane tree shades hellebores, trilliums, two giant fatsias, and European ginger.

It's a garden that is never static.

"I had a visitor to my garden say to me, 'How can you bear to leave this? How can you even leave to go grocery shopping?' It was very funny," she says. "All my gardens have a serenity about them. There is a kind of harmony and there is a definite feel to them. It's not something I was aware of when I first started doing this."

BIRGIT PISKOR'S GARDEN
570 Niagara Street (1908)

Birgit Piskor moved into the Edwardian house in James Bay with her family in 1965. At that time, the garden consisted of a honeysuckle hedge, a white lilac bush, a couple of plum trees, and some conifers she and her dad eventually planted. The most interesting feature was the original concrete checkerboard patio from the 1920s. Her father, a German toolmaker, lived in the house until 1992 before moving and renting it out. When Birgit moved back several years later, the garden was overgrown and neglected.

Birgit knew nothing about plants, but she was driven to build a garden. There was some family history. Her mother had the first large-scale organic market garden on Vancouver Island in the 1980s and her paternal grandfather was a fruit and vegetable gardener in his native Germany. So she experimented with various plants, digging them up when they'd reached a few inches and replanting them somewhere else.

"I just started in the backyard and became obsessed. It was all I did for four years," she says. "I was like a mad thing possessed. It was all I thought about."

Birgit drove her truck to Shawnigan Lake and filled it with red alder. She built the fence first, adding trellises and later the open arbours. Soon rambling roses and clematis grew up along the fence, while golden hop vine and Japanese forest grass added splashes of colour.

Although the garden brimmed with tall, airy blue vervain (pale lilac flowers reaching to 3.4 metres [11 feet] tall), giant feather grass, towering spikes of foxglove, lobelia, hosta, shrubs, and perennials, it still didn't feel complete.

"What was missing was the sculpture element, so I looked around to buy something and there was a lot of cheap, crappy cast stuff like mushrooms and Buddhas and gnomes," she says. "I'd already worked in concrete in the garden and I thought I'd try my hand at sculpting and turns out I have a bit of a flair for it."

Birgit gradually added a fountain, flower sculptures, and *Joy Woman* (a nude with hands that reach up to the sky) to adorn the garden and add height and interest.

At one side of the house, Birgit created a 9-by-1-metre (30-by-3-foot) mosaic path from pebbles that she hand-picked from the beach at Beacon Park. Much later, she discovered that it was the same beach where Emily Carr dug her blue clay when she began designing First Nations pottery to sell to tourists.

In the third year of building her garden, Birgit had a setback. Vandals trashed the front arbour at the entrance to the house. "I just felt so violated because my soul and my sweat and my blood went into the garden. The garden is really the inside of my head spewing out," she says. "I decided to leave the arbour lying crushed on the sidewalk and I made three big signs with red paint that said 'Vandals did this—shame on you' and just left it up for the day."

(top) Birgit Piskor created her arbour from red alder gathered at Shawnigan Lake. EVE LAZARUS PHOTO

(bottom) Birgit Piskor created a mosaic path from pebbles that she hand-picked from the beach at Beacon Park. EVE LAZARUS PHOTO

A few days later, dozens of people started to drop by the house. Two older ladies with walkers brought cards about how much the garden meant to them and to not give up, others offered money, and some offered to help put everything back together.

"It was really remarkable and a real eye-opener for me in terms of what the garden meant to the world out there, not just to me."

In 2005, *Canadian Gardening* named Birgit's garden "the best urban garden in Canada."

Birgit Piskor created a sculpture she calls Joy Woman to add height and interest to her James Bay garden.
EVE LAZARUS PHOTO

BRIAN AND JENNIFER ROGERS'S GARDEN
1883 Gonzales Avenue (ca. 1900)

Brian and Jennifer Rogers have always loved old houses and their history. Brian's grandfather, Benjamin Tingley Rogers, built two heritage mansions that still stand—Gabriola in Vancouver's West End and Shannon in Marpole. The Rogers lived in an old farmhouse on a half acre of land in Kerrisdale before Brian retired from BC Sugar, and they packed up their plants and moved to Victoria.

When they saw the century-old carriage house in 1998, they immediately grasped the potential hidden under the blackberry bushes, bluebells, and a 9-metre-high (30-foot-high) laurel hedge. It took Brian two months to remove all the laurel, then they wheelbarrowed in 68 yards of soil and began to create their garden.

Guy and Sarah Audain had bought the five-acre estate in 1908. The main house, which they called "Ellora," is a chalet designed by Samuel Maclure that faces onto Foul Bay Road. Major Audain met his wife, "Byrdie," one of James Dunsmuir's daughters, on a stopover in Victoria in 1901. The Audains lived at Ellora until about 1922. In 1955, the Christian Science Church bought the house and converted it into a nursing home.

Brian believes his house—originally the Audains' stable—was built in 1901. It's been gradually added onto over the years, and is now an attractive, grey, two-storey cedar-shingled carriage house.

The Audains added accommodation for their gardener in the former hay loft, now an upstairs bedroom. The house became a nurses' residence during World War I, and Brian believes the estate was carved up and his house sold privately sometime in the 1940s. Brian and Jennifer's chunk of the estate is around a third of an acre on an irregular lot—narrower in the front and widening out at the back.

Over the years, one owner built a small cottage in the garden for his art studio. The next owner connected the studio to the main house, and the studio is now the Rogers's bedroom.

Not long after they moved in, Brian pulled down a wall that divided the hallway from the dining room. He found whitewashed wood beams, iron-forged nails, and old hammers. When they were digging through the floor in the dining room, they found the original fir and marks where horse hoofs had dug in around the knots.

The Rogers inherited a black walnut tree in the backyard that Brian believes was brought out from Montreal by Sir Henri-Gustave Joly de Lotbinière, the Lieutenant-Governor of BC in 1900. The massive tree joins giant Douglas fir trees and three huge, century-old apple trees.

There are cherry trees, rhododendrons, ferns, and hostas, and depending on the season, rose-coloured trillium, hellebores, cyclamen, peonies, and lilies. A slate flagstone path bordered with planters of geraniums and fuchsias leads to the house, and to a patio covered in wisteria and passion-fruit vines.

"We try to make it so there is something blooming all year around," says Brian. "My wife is the real plants person and I'm the grunt, but I enjoy the weeding, and I enjoy the pruning and I enjoy cutting things back when that has to be done. It's a labour of love."

Brian says people tell him the garden is peaceful—"a bit of tranquillity."

"It's very restful on the eye," he says. "We don't have any Fuji type of moment. Colour is not hitting you in the face—it's a subtle blend of everything."

Brian and Jennifer Rogers have created a garden around their century-old stable designed by Samuel Maclure.
EVE LAZARUS PHOTO

CHAPTER 8

Bright Lights

OF FILM

For a short time during the Depression, Victoria was Hollywood North. The local industry shot the first Canadian all-talkie movie here and then a string of B movies with titles such as *Across the Border* (with Rita Hayworth), *Death Goes North* (with Rin Tin Tin), and *Secrets of Chinatown* (with Nick Stuart and Lucille Browne). The industry hoped to take advantage of a British quota restriction on foreign films, helped along with a fat investment from Kathleen Dunsmuir, a wealthy daughter of coal-mining baron James Dunsmuir. Kathleen wanted to launch an acting career or, at least, become a Hollywood mogul. Turned out the films weren't guaranteed a shot in UK cinemas after all, and the company failed.

One well-known actor of the time, Arthur Kerr, who was cast as a villain in several movies including *Tugboat Princess* and *Gunsmoke*, lived in 1932 in a three-storey Arts and Crafts house at 36 Howe Street in Fairfield. Current owner Vincent Rickard has lived there for more than 20 years. He didn't know about Kerr, but says that he bought the 1911 house from a prominent church deacon. Other local actors of that era included Reginald Norton Hincks, who appeared in all 12 films shot by Central Films, and Arthur Legge-Willis, who hit the big screen in seven movies. Both lived on Tudor Avenue, at Ten Mile Point just blocks away from where Atom Egoyan and his sister Eve, a concert pianist, grew up. Atom now lives in Toronto, but he was raised in Victoria and attended Mount Douglas Secondary School (as did both Nelly Furtado and David Foster), and went on to earn two Oscar nominations for his films *The Sweet Hereafter* and *Ararat*.

But long before Foster, Furtado, and Egoyan became internationally known, Nell Shipman had already carved out her own impressive career and was, in fact, British Columbia's first filmmaker of note.

(opposite) Nell Shipman wearing a parka for a publicity shot ca.1918.
NELL SHIPMAN COLLECTION, BOISE STATE UNIVERSITY LIBRARY, SPECIAL COLLECTIONS

(below) Arthur Kerr, cast as a villain in several movies shot in Victoria in the 1930's lived at 36 Howe Street.
PHOTO COURTESY VINCENT RICKARD

Helen Foster-Barham (aka Nell Shipman) was born in Victoria in 1892. The family lived in James Bay until 1901.
EVE LAZARUS PHOTO

NELL SHIPMAN (1892—1970)

69 Menzies Street

The dilapidated purple house at the corner of Menzies and Rithet Streets was once the home of Nell Shipman, a Victoria-born actress, screenwriter, producer, and animal trainer.

Born Helen Foster-Barham, this star of the silent screen lived here from her birth in 1892 until 1895 with father Arnold, mother Rose, and older brother Maurice. That year the family moved to Beacon Street, next to Samuel Maclure and his family.

Nell's parents moved to Victoria from England after Arnold, the handsome oldest son, gave up his rights in the family's pottery works. He preferred, wrote Nell in her autobiography *The Silent Screen and My Talking Heart,* to undertake all sorts of other "chancy schemes," while living off some estate money from England.

In the 1892 city directory Arnold is listed as a cannery manager. By 1893, he had reinvented himself as an architect and the following year as a bookkeeper. By 1897, he is listed as the manager for the BC Pottery Company and living at Beacon Street.

At one point, during what Nell describes as a period of extreme poverty, her mother told her that after losing out on several "big opportunities," Arnold took a job as a carpenter. "He swore at me," she told Nell. "Came into the house drunk and said: 'Rose, I hope you're satisfied. On this day I have built a God damn shithouse!'"

Rose managed the house, cooked, did the washing and scrubbing, and had the two children educated in private schools, all on $100 a month.

"[Rose] held her afternoon at-home elegantly, as befitted a lady of her class, kept chickens, a garden, carried her head high beneath the flowery hats of the period, was presented to the Prince and Princess of Wales on a world tour and was always a sweet-smelling, Pear's Soap creature, faithful to the Episcopalian Church she attended, prayer-book in white gloved hand, wisp of lace handkerchief peeking, gold watch pinned to her immaculate shirtwaist," writes Nell.

By the time they'd moved to the little red house on Beacon Street, Maurice had a pony, Nell a bike.

"The cloth for our clothing, tailored in Victoria's Chinatown, came from London. We owned pets and played with children of our own class," she writes. "Our English was clipped and correct."

When Rose received a small inheritance in 1901, the family bought a house on Rockland Avenue and, for the first time, had their own phone. The choice was that or electricity, writes Nell. The 1902 city directory shows a listing for Arnold as retired.

The family moved to Seattle in 1905, and after briefly attending Seattle Grammar, Nell left school at 13 to become an actress.

Years of slogging around in cheap hotels, with stops from Alaska to New York, eventually paid off when in 1910 Nell met her future husband and business partner, Ernest Shipman, a 39-year-old theatrical manager and promoter.

The Shipmans moved to Los Angeles, formed a film production company, and began to cash in on the burgeoning motion picture industry. Nell's career as a leading actress took off, with her portraying strong, adventurous women in outdoorsy movies. Outside of acting, her writing was also in demand.

The Shipmans had a son, Barry. Before divorcing in 1920, they made *Back to God's Country*, a creative and financial success, as well as making Nell one of the first women of film to do a nude scene.

Although Nell's professional life was soaring—she wrote the screenplay for films that would star Cary Grant and Myrna Loy—her personal life was a mess. She married three more times, but by 1963 was broke enough to apply to the Motion Picture Relief Fund for assistance. She was refused.

She died alone in 1970 in Cabazon, California. She was 78.

Although not a filmmaker, Victoria's Spoony Sundher was involved in the entertainment industry and made a different kind of impact on Hollywood with his opening of the Hollywood Wax Museum.

SPOORAN "SPOONY" SINGH SUNDHER (1922–2006)

3210 Bellevue Road

When Spoony and Chanchil Sundher wanted to buy property in Saanich in 1947, the property exclusion laws for non-whites at the time prevented them from doing so. But Spoony had found the ideal site for his house high on a hill on Bellevue Road and had a friend put the lot in his name.

"It wasn't a great area. At that time, it was out of town, but my husband wanted to have that lot because of the beautiful view," says Chanchil. "He was a man with many ideas."

Spoony started building the white modern-style house, but he ran out of money and didn't finish until 1954.

People thought the flat roof odd, but even stranger, says Chanchil, was the form the house took. "He was working in a shingle mill loading shingles onto box cars, so you would have thought he would have wanted to have a traditional house where he could get shingles at a reasonable price, but he didn't want that."

Spoony and Chanchil were both born in India, but moved to Victoria when they were young children. Spoony left Victoria High at 17 to help support the family by working in sawmills and lumber camps, and married Chanchil in an arranged marriage in 1943.

"When we were getting ready to be married, he told his parents that he wasn't going to marry anyone until he met her," Chanchil says. "And the reason he said that was because he had a turban and beard, and he wanted to make sure that was okay with me. He was the kind of person who could convince you of anything—if there was a black tablecloth, he could convince you it was white."

In 1965 Spoony Sundher rode an elephant down Hollywood Boulevard to promote his newly opened wax museum.
PHOTO COURTESY OF TEJ SUNDHER

Spoony and Chanchil Sundher.
Spoony once told a reporter:
"On Hollywood Boulevard dignity
kind of gets lost in the shuffle."
PHOTO COURTESY TEJ SUNDHER

By the time they bought the Bellevue Road property, Spoony also owned the Acme Sawmill at Plumper Bay near Esquimalt. He opened an amusement park in Esquimalt with a gas station and coffee shop, and had the go-carts built using motors from chainsaws to make them faster.

By 1965, Spoony had sold his interest in both the sawmill and the amusement park and was out of a job when he was approached by two friends who were looking for a partner to build a wax museum on Hollywood Boulevard in Los Angeles.

"My husband mortgaged our house, borrowed some money, and took a chance," says Chanchil.

At heart, Spoony was a flamboyant showman. That first year in LA he rode an elephant down Hollywood Boulevard to promote the wax museum, "At that time there weren't many Indian people in Hollywood, and with his turban and beard he was a very imposing figure," says Chanchil.

On opening day, the lineup was half a mile long to get into the museum.

By 1965, the couple had six children, and Chanchil stayed in Victoria for another year, while their oldest son, Meva, 18, finished high school. The family moved to California, and Meva stayed behind to study teaching and eventually became principal of Mount Douglas Secondary in 1998.

The Sundhers owned the Bellevue Road house until the early 1980s.

In 1991, the family opened the Guinness World Records Museum across the street in the old Hollywood Theater, then another wax museum in Branson, Missouri, and branched into land development, farming, and warehousing.

Meva's son, Tej, moved to LA from Victoria in 1999 and is a partner in the family businesses.

Tej says people just can't get enough of celebrities, even if they are wax. His grandfather, he says, was an amazing promoter, holding public relations events starring Sonny and Cher, and doing crazy stunts in the museum, whether that was dressing employees like London Bobbies, sending out skateboarders in gorilla suits to cruise in front of the museum, or having his people jump out from behind wax figures to scare the customers.

In an interview with the *Los Angeles Times* in 1970, Spoony told a reporter, "On Hollywood Boulevard dignity kind of gets lost in the shuffle."

Spoony's death from heart failure at his Malibu home in October 2006 rated a string of lengthy obituaries in newspapers ranging from the *Los Angeles Times* and the *New York Times*, to *USA Today* and the *Globe and Mail*.

"He would have been surprised," says Chanchil.

The Sundher's Bellevue Road house completed in 1954.
EVE LAZARUS PHOTO

And while Nell Shipman and Spoony Sundher both made an impact in Hollywood, Victoria-born David Foster owns the key to the city.

DAVID FOSTER
3915 Ascot Drive

When the Fosters sold their Saanich home in 1972, David Foster, 23, was already making his mark on the global music industry with his band Skylark's hit single "Wildflower."

David grew up in the house that his dad, Morry, a superintendent at the Saanich Municipal Yard, had built for David, his mother, Eleanor, and his six sisters.

The current homeowner found out about her house's famous history when the Victoria-born superstar showed up at the door one afternoon to visit.

David, says the current owner, drops by to visit every four or five years.

111

(above) Ruth, the oldest Foster, says her brother and all five of her sisters remain good friends with the people from Ascot Drive. PHOTO COURTESY OF THE RAY WILLISTON FAMILY CA.1950S

(below) Russell Holmes, David Foster, Dougy Holmes at Ascot Drive. "The house that I grew up in on Ascot Drive and the old neighbourhood means so much to me," says David Foster. "It was a very important part of my life that always stuck with me." PHOTO COURTESY OF THE RAY WILLISTON FAMILY

"David comes to check it out every so often. He likes to come back to the house just to see if the place is still standing," she says. "His sisters Ruth, Jeanie, and Maureen live in Victoria and pop over as well. They seem to be happy with the way we look after the house, so that's the main thing."

Morry started building the three-bedroom home in 1949, the year David was born. The family rented nearby for a while, then moved into the basement while Morry finished the rest of the house. Ruth, the oldest Foster sibling, remembers using the big laundry tub as the kitchen sink. Later, the basement became David's room.

In May 2012, David's sisters planned an Ascot Drive reunion.

"David was doing a fundraiser in Victoria last November, and some of the old Ascot Drive folks and neighbours were there," says Ruth. "David and his wife Yolanda were excited to see them and asked me to round up as many of the old kids from the 'hood as I could and follow them to their new home in Victoria. We made a caravan drive through downtown streets and all traipsed into their home and laughed and talked to the wee hours of the morning. Then David suggested that we do a full-blown Ascot Drive reunion."

Ruth says the great thing is that all seven Foster siblings are still good friends with nearly all the people who once lived on their old street.

"My house that I grew up in on Ascot Drive and the old neighbourhood mean so much to me," says David. "It was a very important part of my life that always stuck with me."

David's music career launched at the age of four when his mother was dusting the piano in the living room. Eleanor hit one of the notes and young David called out, "That's an E." Eleanor called Morry, a piano player who loved music and who quickly realized that his son had perfect pitch. David started piano lessons, and as a teenager performed in local bands and clubs around Victoria including the Old Forge, now Legends on Douglas Street. Morry died in 1968 from a heart attack at 54.

"My upbringing resulted in a huge sense of responsibility and conscientiousness," says Ruth. "Besides our share of the household chores, all seven of us always had a job—babysitting, daffodil picking, strawberry picking, waitressing. David at 13 actually had his own band, was arranging his own music, doing the payroll, and running that business. He never seemed to be a child—always a leader and a team player, working, practising his piano lessons, and telling me how to play my music pieces, correcting me at age five, even though I was eight years his senior!"

"Every week David would ride his bike to his piano teacher's house on Quadra Street," adds Colleen (Jaymes), the youngest Foster sibling.

After Skylark broke up, David stayed in Los Angeles, working as a studio musician with artists such as Michael Jackson, George Harrison, Rod Stewart, and Barbra Streisand. As a record producer, songwriter, and arranger, he's worked with an A-list cast of recording artists including the late Whitney Houston, Michael Bolton, Chicago, Earth, Wind and Fire, Madonna, Nicole Kidman, Celine Dion, Michael Bublé, and Seal.

He retains a strong connection to his hometown. The David Foster Foundation is headquartered in Victoria and holds various celebrity concert galas, which David hosts and directs, as well as tennis and baseball events to raise money and provide emotional support for the families of children needing organ transplants.

"The truth is my sisters are so incredible that I would definitely attribute a lot of my success to their great character and their support over the years," says David. "Our mother, Eleanor, sewed all of our clothes and ran a great household on minimum money. She was very proud of all seven of her kids, not just me."

Colleen has worked with David as his right hand for the past 20 years. Marylou is a successful music coordinator for big movies like *Forrest Gump* and also lives in Los Angeles. Jeanie and Ruth went into nursing, with Ruth dedicating much of her career to terminally ill cancer patients. Maureen also stayed in Victoria and was an administrator for Chew Excavating Ltd. for 38 years. Barbara forged a successful career in real estate in Vancouver.

(above) "The truth is my sisters are so incredible that I would definitely attribute a lot of my success to their great character and support," says David Foster.
PHOTO COURTESY OF THE RAY WILLISTON FAMILY

(below) David and his sisters still drop by the house their father Morry built on Ascot Drive.
PHOTO COURTESY OF THE RAY WILLISTON FAMILY

When David visits the family house, he'll point out things from his youth. "It's really interesting to walk through with him and hear why there are funny little things in funny little places," says the current owner.

For years, she says they couldn't figure out why there was a small rectangular space cut out in the downstairs recreation room. "I said to him one day, 'What is this?' He said his father put the projector on the other side so they could watch home movies."

Morry was the filmmaker of the family, proudly showcasing his large family. "His home movies are so professional," says David. "He took 50 feet of film every week and we have every one of us growing up on film from year to year. What a gift."

AND LITERATURE.

While Victoria has produced more than its share of stars, it also has inspired a wide range of poets, authors, and journalists.

BRUCE HUTCHISON (1901—1992)

Rockhome, 810 Rogers Avenue

In 1924, William Bruce Hutchison bought a dozen acres of "cheaply purchased meadow, rock and trees" from George Rogers, a Saanich dairy farmer.

He hired a plowman to break the sod for a vegetable garden and Dick the digger to hand-dig a hole for the basement of the house. Then he paid two Scottish carpenters $7 a day to build it.

"They mixed by hand the concrete for the massive foundation walls, selected the lumber, haggling over its price, fashioned all the cupboards and bookcases to save the cost of mill work and finished the whole job in three months," he writes in *A Life in the Country*.

The total cost for the eight rooms and two bathrooms was $10,000.

Bruce, his new wife Dorothy, and his mother Constance and father John moved into the Arts and Crafts house, a few miles from Bruce's job at the *Victoria Times*, on a winding gravel road with their closest neighbour a half mile away.

John designed a nursery on the property and called it Rockhome Gardens.

To journalists, Bruce Hutchison is a rock star. An award-winning author, newspaper editor, and friend of prime ministers and Supreme Court justices, he is one of the most influential Canadians of the 20th century. During his life, he notched up three Governor General's Awards for his books, three national newspaper awards, and four honorary university degrees; was made an officer of the Order of Canada; and had a library named after him.

Peter C. Newman called him "the dean of Canadian political commentators," and it's a nod to his ability that, decades before email and the internet, he edited the *Winnipeg Free Press* (1944–1950) and the *Vancouver Sun* (1963–1979) largely by phone and through the post from his home on Vancouver Island.

John Hutchison died in the mid-1930s from lung cancer, and Edith McDiarmid, Dorothy's mother, joined the family at Rockhome. Bruce and Dorothy's daughter Joan was born in 1928 and son Robert three years later.

"My mother was the story of that house," says Robert. "I was probably spoiled by having two grandmothers and a mother, but it was quite a household and my mother managed it all."

The Hutchisons added an upstairs addition with a room for Edith and a den for Bruce. Edith died in 1949 and Constance lived for another 20 years, seeing her hundredth birthday and still reading three newspapers a day.

Bruce Hutchison built Rockhome
in 1924. Alex Barta photo (1981)

As a boy, Robert remembers riding his bike the few miles to Cloverdale School
every day, roaming around the country, counting the sticklebacks in the ditch near
the house, and watching the farmers milk the cows and make butter at the adjacent
Rogers's farm.

"I can remember George [Rogers] senior with his beard, coming down and kick-
ing me out of the barn because I'd be sliding down the haystacks. It was a great place
to grow up," he says.

A natural athlete, Robert joined the Canadian track team and went on to rep-
resent Canada in the 1952 Olympics in Helsinki, Finland. During the summers he
worked at the *Victoria Times* with Denny Boyd on the sports pages, went to the University of Washington on an athletic scholarship to study journalism, graduated instead with a degree in economics, and went on to study law, eventually becoming a
justice of the Supreme Court of BC.

"I decided it was going to be too difficult to try and fill my father's footsteps," he says.

Dorothy died in 1969 in a car accident in Ottawa. Joan and her two teenage sons, Ross and Bruce, moved back into Rockhome.

The house had its share of well-known visitors over the years. Robert remembers sitting around the dining room table as his mother served her famous roasts to John Owen Wilson, chief justice of the Supreme Court; to writers Peter C. Newman and Pierre Berton; to Yousef Karsh, the celebrated portrait photographer; and to artist Mary Bundy and her husband, William Bundy, a code breaker at Bletchley Park during World War II and later foreign policy adviser to US presidents John F. Kennedy and Lyndon B. Johnson.

"The conversation around his dinner table was really fascinating," says Robert. "My father was a great talker and a great cross-examiner. I wish I was as good at cross-examining people."

Bruce lived in the house until his death in 1992. Robert's son, Jim, also a lawyer, took care of his grandfather and stayed on in the house, raising his two children—the fifth generation of Hutchisons to live there.

Robert says that after his father died in 1992, he cleaned out his papers and was staggered by the sheer volume of writing he had produced, particularly during the Depression years.

"He'd write for two or three hours in the morning, go to the office, and then he'd come home and garden in the afternoon," says Robert. "At night he'd read the *New York Times*, the *Globe and Mail*, and all the papers. I can still see him—he'd circle something with pencil, rip it out, and throw it on the living-room floor. He'd do that for about an hour and when he had five pieces of paper on the floor, he'd have his editorials and columns for the next morning."

Most of the land was subdivided in the 1990s by Hutchison's grandsons Bruce and Ross Meek, and a portion of the land was dedicated to the District of Saanich for a park and nature trail. At the time of writing, the family had plans to sell the house. It has a heritage designation, so it's safe from demolition, but as Bruce Meek says, "It is a charming old place in need of a lot of work."

SUSAN MUSGRAVE
North Saanich Tree House

Susan Musgrave, the internationally renowned poet, splits her time between her bed and breakfast—the Copper Beech House on Haida Gwaii—and the eccentric-looking tree house that she owns near Sidney on Vancouver Island.

"I don't understand people who move into key-ready homes that are devoid of personality," she says.

In 1987, Susan fell in love with the house that's built around a 58-metre (190-foot) Douglas fir tree. "When I went in that day, an eagle had landed in the tree and a piece of eagle down came floating down," she says. "I knew it was the house. It just felt so right."

Susan has written more than 20 books, including the poetry collection *What the Small Day Cannot Hold: Collected Poems 1970–1985*, the novel *Cargo of Orchids* (2003), and *You're in Canada Now, Motherfucker: A Memoir of Sorts* (2005).

Her biography describes how she first met Robin Skelton—writer, poet, professor, artist, and male witch—when she was committed to the local psych ward at age 16. "You're not mad," he told her after reading her poetry, "you're a poet."

Susan published her first book of poetry, *Songs of the Sea Witch*, three years later. In 1975, she married Jeffrey Green, a criminal defence lawyer.

Green was one of five lawyers hired to defend a bunch of American and Colombian accused drug smugglers. Susan says that she fell in love with Paul Nelson, one of the defendants, "from across the courtroom." They ran away to Mexico after his acquittal and had daughter Charlotte in 1982.

While Susan was the University of Waterloo's writer-in-residence from 1983 to 1985, Nelson was sent to jail for a previous smuggling charge and, while there, found the Lord. Susan divorced him and soon after received a manuscript from convicted bank robber Stephen Reid, who was serving a 20-year sentence at Millhaven Penitentiary in Ontario. She married Reid at the jail, and on his release in 1987, they moved into Susan's 84-square-metre (900-square-foot) tree house. Their daughter Sophie was born in 1989.

Shortly after they moved in, Robin Skelton arrived to bless their new home. Susan did some research into her home and discovered that it had been built in 1929 by poet Ernest Fern. A neighbour told her that pieces of Emily Carr's Klee Wyck pottery were discovered in the attic by another owner, pieces perhaps left by the artist

when she visited long ago. Other residents included an old lady, who made herbal remedies for the locals, and a boat builder, who instead of fixing the leaking roof, filled it with roofing tar from the inside.

"The whole house creaks in the wind. It's like being on a boat and the roots are the foundation of the house," Susan says. "I absolutely love the house because it's kind of like me—lopsided and wearing down."

In 1999, Stephen Reid became headline material once again when he was arrested for bank robbery following a shootout and car chase through Beacon Hill Park. He was released from prison on day parole in 2008.

Over the years, they have added rooms, but the feeling of privacy remains. Recently, Susan's daughter moved in with her two small children.

"I imagine it's a house that will always be in my dreams," says Susan. "It's a really magical place."

ALICE MUNRO
1648 Rockland Avenue

In 1966, Sheila Munro was 13 and living with her family in a sweet little rented house at 105 Cook Street when she saw an ad for a mansion in Rockland. The asking price was $33,000.

"I guess my father and I had these dreams of grandeur," she says. "The thing was these mansions weren't really popular at that time. People wanted 1960s suburbia."

Jim Munro, owner of Munro's Books, managed to raise $20,000, and his offer was accepted by the owners of the Tudor Revival.

It was love at first sight for Jim and his daughters, but wife Alice, then pregnant with Andrea, was not so enamoured.

"She adjusted to it, but it wasn't her kind of thing. She made me promise that I would do all the vacuuming," says Sheila. "I spent hours vacuuming every Saturday morning. It's a big house."

Short-story writer Alice Munro is one of Canada's most famous authors, but her connection to Victoria is less well known. She moved to the city in 1963 with then-husband Jim Munro and their two oldest daughters, Sheila and Jenny, and set up her table and typewriter in the upstairs "workroom." The room housed the family's washer and dryer, but it was also large and bright with windows that looked out onto garden views to the east and west.

"She has never had an office, ever," says Sheila. "Still doesn't have one."

Alice wrote *Dance of the Happy Shades*—a 1968 Governor General's Award winner—in the workroom. She followed that with her bestselling *Lives of Girls and Women*. In 1973, *Something I've Been Meaning to Tell You* came, a year after her divorce and move back to Ontario.

Sheila remembers some amazing parties and literary figures in the house. Once Margaret Atwood dropped by. "I remember that we sat on the floor cross-legged and she did my horoscope," she says. "She had long curly hair and dressed in a hippyish way."

Other friends of her mother's came by when they were in town. Audrey Thomas and Dorothy Livesay both visited the house. "They were all writing about women's experiences in a way that hadn't been done before," says Sheila. "P.K. Page used to come into the bookstore and meeting her was so exciting for my mother—these people who were not conventional housewives."

Although no records exist, the Rockland Avenue house was most likely designed by architect Francis Rattenbury, as claimed by his daughter. The land was split off from the Rocklands estate, owned by Henry and Clara Dumbleton. The Dumbletons then presented the house, which they named Newholme, to their son Alan Southey Dumbleton, a barrister from South Africa, but they made the unusual step of putting the house in his young wife Mabel's name.

Malcolm Bruce Jackson and his wife Lilian bought the house in 1908. Jackson, a lawyer, well-known liberal supporter and unsuccessful MLA was a close friend of Attorney General Alexander Manson, who in 1924, was charged with investigating the Janet Smith murder case. Smith, a 23-year-old Scottish nanny was found shot in the head by a .45 calibre automatic revolver in the basement of 3851 Osler Avenue in the upmarket Shaughnessy Heights area. The murder rocked Vancouver's elite. It touched on high-level police corruption, kidnapping, drugs, rumoured society orgies, and rampant racism.

Initially Smith's death was ruled a suicide, but public pressure forced further investigation into the case. Her body was exhumed, a second inquest held, and

Alice Munro in the front garden of the home on Rockland Avenue in 1968.
PHOTO COURTESY SHEILA MUNRO

Manson appointed Jackson as his special prosecutor.

Suspicion fell on Wong Foon Sing, a Chinese servant who worked for the Bakers, the family who employed Smith as their nanny. During the investigation, Wong was kidnapped by men dressed in Ku Klux Klan robes and hoods, taken to a house where he was kept for six weeks and beaten and tortured in an attempt to get a confession. In one of the many bizarre turns in the case, Jackson was eventually charged with complicity in the kidnapping.

Jackson died in 1947 and Lilian remained in the house until her death in 1950.

By the time the 1960s came around, the house had been turned into a duplex and was in rough shape, but Jim could see the potential. The gardens had once been beautiful, and inside, the house has five fireplaces under 3.7-metre (12-foot) ceilings, and a nanny's quarters, which became bedrooms for Sheila and Jenny, with a separate staircase to the kitchen.

In 1977, Jim married textile artist Carole Sabiston in what the family called the "chapel" because of the stained-glass effect Jim had painted around the windows, and for his old pump organ that still sits under the staircase. Jim played Purcell's *Trumpet Volunteer* on the organ before the wedding, which was attended by daughters Sheila and Andrea, Carole's parents, and her son Andrew Sabiston, now an actor and writer.

Carole says that the official term for her work is textile assemblage—"assembled fabric that's stitched all over the surface creating a new surface," but that seems such a simplification of her work: art that is full of multiple layers of netting, matte, leather, cotton, silk, brocade, and lace.

Her commissions include the giant Sunburst for the EXPO '86 opening ceremony in Vancouver, and her work *Commonwealth Cape of Many Hands* featured in the closing ceremony of the 1994 Commonwealth Games. She received the Order of British Columbia in 1992.

In the late 1970s, Carole added a studio that is connected to the house by a glazed passage. It was here on the floor of her home studio that she created the dramatic five-panel work of mountains and ocean that hangs in Government House, as well as perhaps her most publicly accessible work: literary-themed murals and eight large banners depicting the seasons that hang in Munro's Books on Government Street.

During the 10 years of the Victoria Literary Festival (1994–2004), Margaret Drabble, Ian McEwan, Vikram Seth, Jane Urquhart, Carol Shields, and Simon Winchester were just a few of the literary giants to visit the Rockland house.

The walls in the main-floor rooms are now painted different shades of terra cotta and warm grays, and serve as a backdrop for the collections that fill the walls, salon-style. A large collection of wearable art—everything from straw hats to cocktail hats to top hats—covers the wall by the front door from floor to ceiling. One corner of the room has a key collection–big iron keys to tiny clock keys picked up by Carole from flea markets around the world. In another corner is a quirky collection of carpet beaters, including the first one Carole bought when she lived in Spain.

Carole was the last member to join the Limners, an eclectic bunch of artists with talents that ranged from painting, sculpture, and collage to printmaking, textile, calligraphy, mixed media, and poetry. It seems about the only thing they had in common was their base in Victoria, their creative genius, and their love of a good party.

(top) Carole Sabiston added a studio to the house in the late 1970s. Murals she created here hang in Government House and Munro's Books. EVE LAZARUS PHOTO

(bottom) Jim Munro played Purcell's *Trumpet Volunteer* on the pump organ shortly before he married Carole Sabiston here in 1977. EVE LAZARUS PHOTO

121

CHAPTER 9

The Limners

The Limners, who took their name from the wandering sign painters and portraitists of early days, held their first meeting in Herbert Siebner's living room in 1971. Over the years, the original group of nine was joined by nine others. Its members were Maxwell Bates, Pat Martin Bates, Richard Ciccimarra, Robert de Castro, Walter Dexter, Nita Forrest, Colin Graham, Helga Grove, Jan Grove, LeRoy Jensen, Elza Mayhew, Myfanwy Pavelic, Carole Sabiston, Herbert Siebner, Robin Skelton, Sylvia Skelton, Karl Spreitz, and Jack Wilkinson.

"We didn't sit around and talk about manifestos, or say 'What is the meaning behind all this?' We were all good friends and our key to this connection was that we respected each other's work, had lively arguments, discussed the need for art in life and how we could find more collectors. Moreover, we enjoyed exhibiting together. There was no competition," says Carole Sabiston.

While several of the artists established international reputations in their field, others exhibited and sold their work across the country, and all 17 helped shape and develop Victoria's art scene.

"It was and is a splendid group of artists, and every member of the group could reasonably be described as just a touch eccentric," writes Robin Skelton in *The Memoirs of a Literary Blockhead*.

The Skeltons hosted an open house every Thursday night for seven years, and these evenings were often attended by as many as a hundred writers, Limners, and various hangers-on. After they stopped, Carole Sabiston continued the Thursday open house in her home for the next two years or so. Other popular gathering spots were Herbert Siebner's Prospect Lake house, Myfanwy Pavelic's studio at Spencerwood, Elza Mayhew's studio at Fisherman's Wharf, and Pat Martin Bates's heritage house, situated within staggering distance of the Skeltons'.

(opposite) The Limners from L to R: Walter Dexter, Carole Sabiston, Karl Spreitz, Myfanwy Pavelic, Colin Graham, Helga Grove, Herbert Siebner, Pat Martin Bates, Jan Grove, LeRoy Jensen, Elza Mayhew, Robin Skelton, Roberto de Castro.
PHOTO COURTESY TIMES COLONIST, 1985

HERBERT SIEBNER (1925–2003)

270 Meadowbrook

Herbert Siebner may just be the biggest name in Victoria's painting history after Emily Carr. Certainly he is one of the most colourful and controversial artists to come out of Vancouver Island's vibrant art scene.

Herbert is known for his painting and murals—his art hangs in collections all over the world—and his oils and lithographs kick-started modernism in Victoria. But he was also multi-faceted, working in everything from scrap metal and concrete to prints, engravings, and serigraphs.

His early works were abstract expressionist in style—colourful landscapes and beach scenes painted in watercolour and ink. He created sensual, hand-coloured lithographs and woodcuts such as the fabulous red and orange nude in *Orgasm*, and he also worked in crayon and silkscreen, even making his own sgraffito tiles for his bathroom at Meadowbrook.

Herbert Siebner loved to dress up, hold wild parties and was always the first to strip.
PHOTO COURTESY ANGELA NIELSEN

When commissioned to paint a mural for the Student Union Building at the University of Victoria, he portrayed all the student activities he could think of except studying.

Born in Stettin, Germany, Herbert was the younger of two boys, growing up in a large apartment shared with several servants.

In 1943, when he was 17, Herbert's cultured life came to a crashing end when he was reluctantly drafted into the war. The following year, bombs destroyed his home.

He studied at the Berlin Academy and married Hannelore, a dancer, in 1950. Their daughter, Angela, was born the next year, and the family immigrated to Victoria. Herbert taught painting and his students included future Limners Karl Spreitz and Nita Forrest.

In 1965, the Siebners bought seven-and-a-half acres of wilderness overlooking Prospect Lake on Meadowbrook Road. The property gave the artist the privacy to do whatever he wanted, and the room to work on large-scale murals and stone figures.

"He was constantly working, he always had a sketch pad with him, and if he happened not to have it when we were out for dinner or visiting friends, he'd playfully sketch people or animals on napkins or matchbook covers," recalls Angela. "What I remember most about Dad is that he loved his life with a passion; his family, his art, and his friends."

Herbert died of heart failure at 78. Hannelore died in 2005 from breast cancer.

Before selling the property in 2011, Angela and her husband, Rene Nielsen, carefully photographed the house and preserved what they could of her father's art and eccentricities.

"The house was a very plain and simple little house, and everybody was always saying, 'Oh Herbert, you need a big place with a big studio,' and he said, 'No. I don't. I just need a place to paint—just leave me alone," says Rene. "He loved life, he loved women, and he loved the freedom of Canada."

He also loved sweet wine and cigars.

"Every time he got a new bottle of wine that he had never had before, he would take the label off and paste it on the kitchen ceiling," says Rene. "There were thousands of them."

Herbert and Hannelore were renowned for wild parties often attended by other members of the Limners and close friends such as Robin Skelton, Karl Spreitz, and the Groves.

"His life was all about doing what he wanted to do, and if he didn't feel like putting clothes on that day, he wouldn't put clothes on that day," says Rene. "Hannelore would always make sure that he had clean underwear on at parties because she knew that he was going to end up peeling off at some point."

Herbert was a prolific writer and painted his basement chimney with whatever came to mind.
PHOTO COURTESY ANGELA NIELSEN

Herbert, who was also a prolific writer, painted a large chimney in his studio basement with whatever came into his mind. His sayings such as "Work is a mistake from which I learn" and "Angst is shit" were printed all over the brickwork.

Robin Skelton writes in *The Memoirs of a Literary Blockhead* of Herbert's penchant for fancy dress, peculiar hats, and masks. "On one occasion [Herbert] brought his pet chicken to a show and it flew up to the ceiling in a cackling frenzy, shedding feathers and hilarity everywhere."

In *A Passion for Art*, Patricia Bovey writes that at any gathering where there was water, Herbert was always the first to strip off his clothes and jump in. The most memorable gathering was at Spencerwood, shortly after the Pavelics had installed an exercise pool, when everybody followed Herbert in creating, what Myfanwy Pavelic told Bovey, looked like a "swirling bowl of macaroni."

MYFANWY PAVELIC (1916–2007)
Spencerwood, 577 Ardmore Road, North Saanich

When Myfanwy Pavelic refused to travel to Montreal to paint Pierre Trudeau's official portrait, the former prime minister came to her.

"He was the most delightful, intelligent and charming house guest I've had," she told the *Times Colonist* in 2000. "We wandered and talked, and sometimes worked 20 hours a day together … In the end, when I had finished, he said how much he liked it. I had, he said, caught and condensed the salient parts of his life."

Myfanwy produced 35 paintings from Trudeau's two visits to Spencerwood, but in the painting that hangs in the House of Commons in Ottawa, and which is featured on a 2001 postage stamp, he is painted in his trademark cape holding his gloves and beret in his hand.

Over the years Myfanwy's guests have included actress Katharine Hepburn, pia-

nist Glenn Gould, and Indian sitarist Ravi Shankar. Her portrait of violinist Yehudi Menuhin hangs in the National Portrait Gallery in London.

"Yehudi was staying with us one time," she told the *Times Colonist*. "I was working in my studio when he popped in with his violin. 'I feel like leaving some music here,' he said. Then lifting up his violin, he started to play."

Myfanwy Pavelic was the only child of John William (Will) Spencer and Lillian Watts, and the granddaughter of David Spencer of Spencer's Department Stores.

Sept. 9.1996 Myfanwy Pavelic
577 Admorc.

Her grandfather's mansion is now the Art Gallery of Greater Victoria at 1040 Moss Street, and she grew up at 1045 Joan Crescent, a rambling house designed by Thomas Hooper in 1918, with Craigdarroch Castle as its neighbour.

Myfanwy had a privileged upbringing. She spent her early life travelling through Europe, studying with private tutors; living at home with a nanny, a French cook, and a gardener; and later attending boarding schools, first near her home in Victoria and then in Montreal. She summered at Spencerwood, the beachfront cottage her father built in 1924. Her mentor, Emily Carr, encouraged her to hold her first exhibition at age 15, and she made her debut in London, where she was introduced to the king and queen.

Although rich and privileged, Myfanwy suffered from a crippling joint disorder that forced her to spend much of her youth confined to braces. She studied piano, and then when told that her wrists weren't strong enough for a concert career, decided to pursue painting full-time.

She married Victoria lawyer Don Campbell at age 23, and her father had 1000 Joan Crescent built as a wedding present. The marriage was short-lived, and after her divorce, she moved to New York and took up residence at the Algonquin Hotel, a famous literary and artistic hangout at the time. It was in New York where she met and married Nikola Pavelic, the son of a high-ranking Yugoslavian cabinet minister. The Pavelics moved back to Spencerwood in 1969.

Myfanwy filled the walls of the house with paintings by Max Bates, Herbert Siebner, Gordon Smith, and Jack Shadbolt.

Victoria artist and writer Robert Amos was working at the Art Gallery of Greater Victoria when he met Myfanwy in the 1970s.

"Victoria in general thought of her as something like nobility. She was the favourite daughter of a very wealthy family and she certainly played the role," he says. "She did not have the common touch."

Myfanwy was charming, full of stories, and very attractive. "I could easily name half a dozen men who fell completely in love with her," he says. "She was still quite a stunning 80-year-old."

Myfanwy Pavelic with her daughter Tessa at her studio at Spencerwood.
ROBERT AMOS PHOTO (1996)

Pierre Trudeau posed for his official portrait here at Spencerwood in 1991. Other guests have included Katharine Hepburn, Glenn Gould, Ravi Shankar and Yehudi Menuhin.
EVE LAZARUS PHOTO

A self-portrait painted in 1989, five years after she was made a Member of the Order of Canada, shows Myfanwy in a side profile, her white hair pulled back in a pony tail, bangs, blue eyes, but missing her trademark goggle-like eyeglasses. Amos remembers that she often wore an unusual colour of green and always had a sweater knotted over her shoulders.

Amos, who is working on a book about Myfanwy, visited her studio at Spencerwood many times over the years. Photographs he took show a big room with a huge beach stone fireplace and soaring ceilings with windows that flooded the room with light. Her own paintings filled the walls, and there was a comfortable sitting area where she would do all her entertaining.

In 1993, Myfanwy donated 364 paintings to the University of Victoria, including 249 of her own and Emily Carr's *Happiness*.

Myfanwy lived at Spencerwood until her death in 2007 at 91. Her daughter, Tessa, died two years later, and the estate went up for sale for $6.8 million.

Myfanwy Pavelic and Elza Mayhew were the only two Limners born in Victoria. Both were born in 1916.

ELZA MAYHEW (1916–2004)

330 St. Lawrence Street

In 1972, Elza Mayhew received the biggest commission of her career—a sculpture for the hundredth anniversary of Prince Edward Island. When finished, *Column of the Sea*, cast in bronze, weighed almost 2,720 kilograms (three tons), soared to 5 metres (16 feet) in height, and took two years to make before reaching its destination at the Confederation Arts Centre in Charlottetown.

At five foot two inches tall, Elza was a petite green-eyed brunette with a vision so original and strong that her work has been compared to that of Henry Moore's.

Elza's early work was mostly made from compound stone. She'd pour the cement into prepared boxes and then carve the stone before it hardened. Later, she cast most of her work in bronze or aluminum, and perfected a method of carving first in Styrofoam. Much later, when she was in her 80s, Elza suffered from a form of deteriorating dementia caused by the toxic fumes from the Styrofoam that she had used for her sculptures.

Elza lived in an apartment in Oak Bay and would spend her working week at the studio, staying in the upstairs loft that contained the bedroom, bathroom, and small built-in Scandinavian-style kitchen.

Anne Mayhew remembers her mother working in her studio, often alongside Robert de Castro, her companion and fellow Limner. "*Column of the Sea* was sliced down the middle and cut into 30 sections, each piece about the size of a dishwasher door," says Anne. "Then she and Bob would hollow out the Styrofoam using saws, knives, and files, and hot irons to melt it, and then sand and shave it as thin as a shell."

Elza studied classics at the University of British Columbia. In 1938, she married childhood sweetheart Alan Mayhew, son of Canada's ambassador to Japan; had two children, Anne and Garth; and lost her young husband in 1943 when the plane he was flying went down in a hurricane over the Indian Ocean during World War II.

In the late 1950s, she studied under Jan Zach and received her Master of Fine Arts in Sculpture from the University of Oregon and began to exhibit and sell her work to galleries, universities, and private collectors. She represented Canada at the prestigious Venice Biennale in 1964, and the University of Victoria awarded her an honorary doctorate in 1989.

Elza Mayhew in her studio creating the Styrofoam mold for *Column of the Sea*.
PHOTO BY KEN MCALLISTER, COURTESY OF ANNE MAYHEW

Anne, a writer and editor, has kept hundreds of her mother's drawings from when
she was at the design stage of her work. She accompanied her mother on several
trips through Europe and once to Yucatan, Mexico, to look at local sculpture. She
says her mother loved languages, music, and Japanese flower arranging, and her
work was inspired by Roman tombstones and Japanese roadside shrines.

After Elza was satisfied with the carvings that she'd made in Styrofoam, they were
taken to the Aluminum and Brass Foundry in Oregon. The foundry specialized in
manufacturing manhole covers, and Elza had to retrain the workers to cast her art.
After the foundry, the pieces were sent over to Myrmo's Machine Shop, a logging-
truck repair business in Eugene, where a section of the shop was reserved for her,
and where she would spend the next few months flanked by at least two assistants.
It was here that Elza cast *Coast Spirit*, a massive bronze 4.9-metre (16-foot) column
for the University of Victoria, and *Concordia*, a bronze column she created for Expo
'67 in Montreal.

Victoria architect Alan Hodgson designed the studio for Elza in 1969. The studio
itself is two floors high with large windows and skylights, and equipped with a hoist
and various blocks and tackles and chains to allow Elza to lift the heavy pieces of
bronze. Hodgson designed one entire wall to slide open, allowing Elza to swing
large pieces of metal weighing up to 545 kilograms (1,200 pounds) out on a hoist
after they'd returned from Eugene, Oregon, or needed to be shipped out to a customer, a gallery, or an exhibition.

When Elza bought the two waterfront properties at Fisherman's Wharf, she also acquired an Italianate house with a widow's walk built in 1892. The studio and the house received a heritage designation from the City of Victoria in 2011, but both look to become victims of demolition through neglect.

PAT MARTIN BATES (1927–)

1344 Victoria Avenue, Oak Bay

In 1971, Pat had just returned to Victoria from a Canada Council Arts Fellowship where she followed the route of Alexander the Great through the Middle East in a Volkswagen camper named Bucephalus. She, husband Al, and daughter Jocelyn were renting a cottage in Oak Bay when Sylvia Skelton called and told her: "Pat, your house is for sale, and it's almost across the street from us. Come and have a look. The Napiers are splendid people and want to sell to people who would love it."

Pat drove by, decided it was too big, too expensive, and just impossible.

"The phone rings again, and it is the real estate agent, who is coming to pick me up to talk to the owners," says Pat. "So we went and the Napiers loved us and we moved in—just like that. The house not only chose us, but demanded us."

At 85, Pat Martin Bates is strikingly beautiful. A bright scarf is wrapped around her dark hair. She's wearing chunky silver jewellery and a jacket full of blues, reds, and purples.

"The house not only chose us, but demanded us," says Pat Martin Bates. EVE LAZARUS PHOTO

"There was always music in this house as I can sense it," says Pat Martin Bates. American consul George A. Bucklin lived here in the early 1930s and was known for his musical evenings.
EVE LAZARUS PHOTO

Pat cuts an exotic figure as she stands in front of her big stone fireplace. When she moved in, it was painted an ugly ochre colour and she spent countless hours down on her hands and knees scraping off the paint left behind from a past resident—once in full evening dress before a New Year's Eve party.

Pat Martin was born in Saint John, New Brunswick, in 1927. She met Clyde Allison (Al) Bates when she was 13 and decided to marry him. "He was unaware of this; in fact, he was unaware of me," she says. But in June 1948, marry him she did.

"When she met me, she said, 'I like your name, but I'm not going to give up mine,' and it became Pat Martin Bates," says Al. "This is 60-odd years ago. It was customary to drop your maiden name, but she refused to."

She started her formal art training at 12 and later studied at art institutes in Belgium, France, and the US. As the wife of a military man, and the mother of two, she lived in Halifax, Antwerp, Ottawa, and Wainwright, Alberta, before settling in Esquimalt in 1963.

The Arts and Crafts house was designed by Fred Wood and built in 1912 for Marshall Pollock Gordon, a one-time reeve of Oak Bay. The house received heritage designation in 1997, and the living room, dining room, and study with the original leaded windows, parquet floors, brass fittings, and fireplace, are listed as heritage interiors.

John Duncan MacLean, a former teacher and school principal, bought the house in 1921. MacLean studied medicine at McGill University, turned to politics, and in 1915 was elected mayor of Greenwood, BC. At the time of purchase, he was minister of education and finance, and he became the premier of BC upon the death of Premier John Oliver in 1927. *The Canadian Encyclopedia* describes MacLean rather unflatteringly as an "unimaginative, colourless premier who took office when his party's fortunes were on the wane." The Liberals were defeated in 1928 and MacLean resigned, became chairman of the Canadian Farm Loan Board, and moved to Ottawa in 1930.

The next resident was American Consul George A. Bucklin. "There was always music in this house as I can sense it," says Pat. "The consul was known for his musical evenings."

The house changed hands several times and became a boarding house during World War II. Before Pat and Al returned it to a single-family home, the house had been turned into a duplex and provided a home to a series of renters, including fellow Limner Carole Sabiston and Richard Simmins, director of the Art Gallery of Greater Victoria.

Over the years, Pat has notched up an impressive international reputation as a contemporary printmaker with a long string of professional designations and accolades, including an honorary doctorate in fine arts from the University of Victoria. She is a Fellow of the Royal Society of Canada and has represented Canada at the Venice Biennale and in Japan, Yugoslavia, Italy, China, Russia, and the Middle East. Pat says mostly she's proud of being the only Canadian to receive the

(top) Pat Martin met Clyde (Al) Bates when she was 13 and decided to marry him. "He was unaware of this; in fact, he was unaware of me," she says. They were married in June 1948.
PHOTO COURTESY PAT MARTIN BATES.

(bottom) When she met me, she said, 'I like your name, but I'm not going to give up mine,'" says Al Bates. Pat and Al's 50th anniversary.
PHOTO COURTESY PAT MARTIN BATES

Every wall, every surface, every nook of Pat Martin Bates' house is covered in art—her own prints and sketches, paintings from fellow Limners, small sculptures, cards, books, bowls and plates.
EVE LAZARUS PHOTO

gold medal in Norway's Graphic Biennial and also the only woman and Canadian to receive the Global Graphics Award from Holland.

Al says that they have never eaten a meal in their dining room, and it's not hard to see why. Every wall, every surface, every nook of the house is covered in art— Pat's prints and sketches, paintings from fellow Limners, or small sculptures, cards, books, bowls, and plates.

Al flicks a switch and a framed lightbox jumps to life, a technique Pat pioneered in the 1960s, now commonly used in backlit outdoor advertising. Pat applies several techniques in a single work: painting, printmaking, and collage. She still uses her grandmother's hat pin to pierce holes in the paper to allow in pinpricks of light.

"She pushed the boundaries beyond multiple-use editions, brought poetry and narrative into the visual arts, and is the backbone behind the Victoria College of Arts," Martin Segger, the former director of the Maltwood Art Museum, told the *Times Colonist* in 2008.

Pat was a professor in the Visual Arts Department at the University of Victoria for more than 30 years.

"Pat arrived in Victoria a year or so after me—a most glorious misfit," writes colleague and fellow Limner Robin Skelton. "For one thing, she was very beautiful with thick, glossy black hair, a superb figure, and a sense of style that made every other woman on campus look dowdy and scared a good many of the men."

ROBIN SKELTON (1925–1997)
1255 Victoria Avenue, Oak Bay

> My home is Victoria and the big house on Victoria Avenue is the very centre
> of my existence. It drew me to it, and it has supported and strengthened me
> ever since I first climbed the steps and entered the white front door.
> – Robin Skelton, *The Memoirs of a Literary Blockhead*

Photographs of Robin Skelton show him as an imposing figure, druid-like with his long beard, flowing white hair, a tattooed wrist, chunky rings on every finger, and a talismanic pentagram around his neck. He looks quite fierce, yet his students, colleagues, and many friends describe him as a tad eccentric, but also kind and humble.

Robin writes: "I am sometimes puzzled to know which hat I am supposed to be wearing when approached by strangers. Am I a poet, an artist, an art critic, a fiction writer, a scholar, an editor, a teacher, a publisher or a witch?"

Born in 1925 in the tiny village of Easington, Yorkshire, England, Robin was all those things and more. He came to Canada in 1963 after a distinguished academic career and a stint during World War II as a codes and ciphers clerk in India. He met his second wife, Sylvia, in 1957, a special education teacher in Cornwall, who was married to the artist Michael Seward Snow. Snow fell in love with Robin's first

wife, Margaret. They divorced, remarried within days of each other, attended each other's weddings, and remained friends for the rest of their lives. Divorce, notes their daughter Brigid Skelton, was not an easy thing in 1950s England, and not something that either couple took lightly. "There was stigma," she says. "The Snows, who remained in England, suffered particularly."

Sylvia was a talented calligrapher. She was a founding member of the Fairbank Calligraphy Society and a member of the Victoria Choral Society for more than 25 years. Brigid remembers her mother practising her parts on a little electric organ in the sunroom at the back of the house.

Robin taught at the University of Victoria for nearly 30 years, was the founding chair of the Creative Writing Department, founded the *Malahat Review*, and wrote art criticism for the local paper. He also worked in collage and sculpture, wrote volumes of poetry, and published more than a hundred books during his lifetime. As a Wiccan, he was one of Canada's most high profile male witches, wrote books about the subject, banished ghosts, and blessed Susan Musgrave's North Saanich tree house when she bought it in 1987.

According to an obituary which appeared online at *ABC BookWorld*, Robin cured Margaret Atwood's arthritis, and was "fond of Irish whisky and flea markets, he never learned to drive a car and he disliked telephones … As poet Linda Rogers put it, it was like living near Merlin."

The Skeltons bought the Oak Bay house in 1971. When Robin and Sylvia looked at the house, they found it had plenty of room for their family of five. Robin writes that he looked around, came down the stairs, and told owner Sandra Hoey that they'd take the house. "I had not even asked the price. Sandra gaped and Sylvia almost fainted. I had to produce $20,000 for the down payment and lawyers fees in 10 days."

The large Edwardian house was designed by Robert Garrow, the same architect behind the Georgia Hotel in Vancouver (1927) and built for lumber merchant Alexander Walter Elliot, who used his wood in the construction of the house. The Elliots lived there until the late 1920s and the Woottons became the house's custodians during the 1930s.

"There was an already shelved study, for the house had once belonged to Judge Wootton, who had his own library. There was a monstrously large basement; there was indeed everything we needed and there was also something more. I knew the house wanted us," writes Robin. "From the very first day that we moved in, it began to alter our lives."

By the 1980s the Skeltons had collected more than 30,000 books; 200 paintings, drawings, and sculptures, many from other Limners; over 2,000 78 rpm records; a collection of stone eggs from all over the world; and the house's ghost: a young Eurasian woman who from time to time still wanders the upstairs corridor.

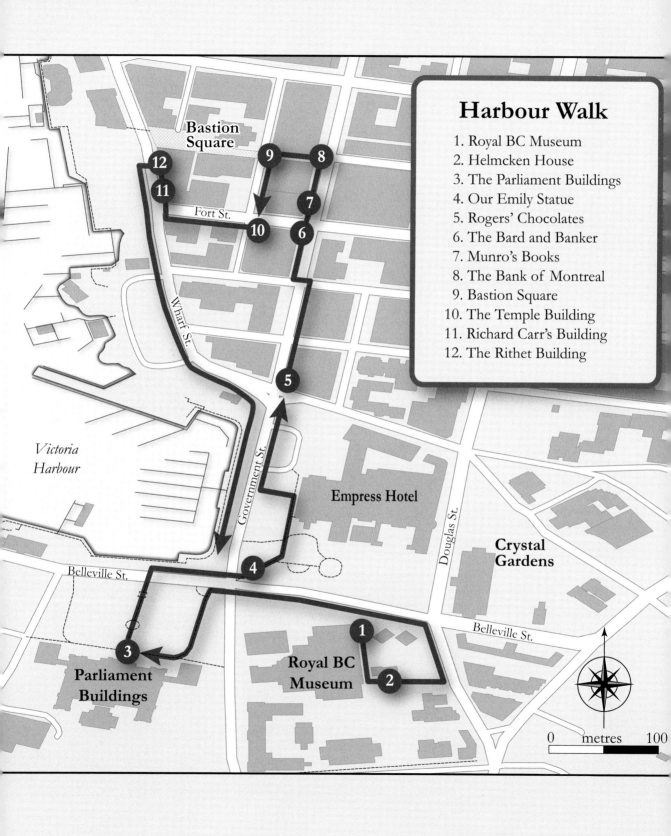

Harbour Walk

1. Royal BC Museum
2. Helmcken House
3. The Parliament Buildings
4. Our Emily Statue
5. Rogers' Chocolates
6. The Bard and Banker
7. Munro's Books
8. The Bank of Montreal
9. Bastion Square
10. The Temple Building
11. Richard Carr's Building
12. The Rithet Building

Bastion Square

12

9   8

11

Fort St.

7

10   6

Wharf St.

5

Victoria Harbour

Empress Hotel

Government St.

Douglas St.

Crystal Gardens

Belleville St.

4

Belleville St.

3

Parliament Buildings

Royal BC Museum

1

2

0   metres   100

CHAPTER 10

A Stroll Around Downtown

Many of the heritage buildings you will see in Victoria were designed by architects who figure prominently throughout this book and who were formative in shaping the city. Today these heritage buildings are filled with boutiques, art galleries, book stores, and cafés.

This chapter will take you on a stroll through the downtown core and back through the Inner Harbour. Spend an hour or the entire day. The Royal BC Museum is a fitting place to start because it's filled with local history, including a town that's replicated from the early 1900s.

The Empress Hotel, ca.1930s.
COURTESY SAANICH ARCHIVES

1) THE ROYAL BC MUSEUM

675 Belleville Street

James Bay is the oldest residential area of Victoria and takes its name from Governor James Douglas, as does Douglas Street. Douglas built his house in the 1850s on the current site of the Royal British Columbia Museum, where the house stood until 1906.

At one time, Belleville Street was lined with mansions. David Spencer, who owned the largest department store in early Victoria, and his wife, Emma, had 13 children and built a large house they called the "Poplars." BC Archives now stands on this property. Robert and Joan Dunsmuir built Fairview (demolished in the 1950s) on the corner of Menzies and Quebec Streets in 1885, and they lived there until they upgraded to Craigdarroch Castle in Rockland.

Sir James Douglas House, early 1900s. COURTESY SAANICH ARCHIVES 1981-019-050

2) HELMCKEN HOUSE

638 Elliott Street

Fortunately, one of the oldest houses built in the province still stands in its original location. Dr. John Sebastian Helmcken, a surgeon, built this single-storey house shortly after arriving in Victoria in 1850. He had planned to stay only a year or two. Instead, he married Sir James Douglas's daughter Cecilia, became a politician, and was one of three men sent to Ottawa in 1870 to negotiate BC's union with the rest of Canada.

Helmcken outlived his wife by more than half a century and lived in the house until his death in 1920 at 96. Helmcken House is now a provincial museum.

Helmcken House. Inset, statue of Dr. J.S. Helmcken. EVE LAZARUS PHOTO

3) THE PARLIAMENT BUILDINGS

501 Belleville Street

One of Victoria's most visible landmarks (especially at night when they light up the sky with 3,300 light bulbs), the Parliament Buildings were designed by 25-year-old Francis Rattenbury, who moved to Victoria in 1892 shortly after winning a design competition against 60 other architects.

Rattenbury continued to place his stamp firmly on the Inner Harbour by designing the Empress Hotel (1908), Crystal Gardens (1925), and the CPR Steamship (1926).

PHOTO COURTESY OF JESSE ADAMS

4) OUR EMILY STATUE

At the Fairmont Empress Hotel

In October 2010, 65 years after her death, Emily Carr was recognized with this $400,000, 313-kilogram (728-pound) bronze statue, dedicated to her memory. The larger-than-life statue looks out over the harbour from the lawn of the Fairmont Empress Hotel at the corner of Belleville and Government Streets.

Sculptor Barbara Paterson, the same artist who created the *Famous Five* statue in Calgary and Ottawa, has seated Emily on a rock, sketchpad in hand, her monkey Woo perched on her shoulder, and her dog Billie by her side.

EVE LAZARUS PHOTO

5) ROGERS' CHOCOLATES

913 Government Street

By the early 1900s, buildings were springing up all over the downtown area. Thomas Hooper, C. Elwood Watkins, and John Teague designed the Rogers' Building in 1903. It's unexciting from the outside, but the art nouveau interior remains virtually untouched. "Rogers'" is printed in mosaic tile work on the floor, beneath the original stained glass and oak panelling.

Local historian John Adams features the building on his ghost tour and bills the national historic site as "Victoria's oldest, most famous and most haunted chocolate shop." The original owners, Charles and Leah Rogers, became quite eccentric after their son Frederick, 15, shot himself in 1905. Adams says the couple, who often slept in the kitchen of their old store, reputedly never left.

EVE LAZARUS PHOTO

6) THE BARD AND BANKER
1022 Government Street

On the other side of Government, past Broughton Street, a stately Italianate Style building erected in 1885 is now a pub called the Bard and Banker. The name would surely have delighted its namesake and one-time resident, Robert Service.

The Scottish-born poet lived in Victoria in the early 1900s and spent some of his 20s working as a bank teller in this building. Service is immortalized in the poems "The Cremation of Sam McGee" and "The Shooting of Dan McGrew."

EVE LAZARUS PHOTO

7) MUNRO'S BOOKS
1108 Government Street

This neo-classical building has housed Munro's Books since 1984, but was originally designed for the Royal Bank of Canada by Thomas Hooper in 1909. Proprietor Jim Munro's first wife, Alice, is the well-known author. His second wife, Carole Sabiston, is a highly regarded fabric artist. Carole's stunning wall hangings are exhibited in the store.

EVE LAZARUS PHOTO

8) THE BANK OF MONTREAL
1200 Government Street

The Irish Times Pub has taken over this building designed by Francis Rattenbury for the Bank of Montreal in 1896.

Rattenbury designed this bank in the chateau style more common to railway stations and hotels rather than the conservative neo-classical style favoured by banks of the day. He did so in part because of the bank's association with the CPR. The stone is from Haddington and Nelson Islands.

9) BASTION SQUARE

Bastion Square was the centre of action in the gold rush days—wild streets filled with bars and saloons. Francis Rattenbury and H.O. Tiedmann, a civil engineer, initially designed the regal old building in 1889 at 28 Bastion Square as the Supreme Court of British Columbia.

The building hosted public executions and the old jailhouse. Its occupants dispensed justice for some 75 years, until 1965 when the building became the Maritime Museum. Current exhibits include the graveyard of the Pacific and the *Tilikum*, originally a cedar dugout canoe. The small boat hasn't sailed for over a century, but it carried the infamous Captain Voss partway around the world in 1901.

EVE LAZARUS PHOTO

10) THE TEMPLE BUILDING

535 Fort Street

Walk down Langley Street to see the Temple Building, designed by Samuel Maclure in 1893. The landmark building with its red terra cotta and red brick design was built for Robert Ward and Co. Insurance. Over the years it has housed law firms, provincial government offices and the Victoria Chamber of Commerce. Lombard Properties bought the building in 2000 and completed a major overhaul and renovation.

EVE LAZARUS PHOTO

11) RICHARD CARR'S BUILDING

1107 Wharf Street

Richard Carr started up his business in 1864 to supply miners on their way to the gold fields. "A fat round stove, nearly always red hot, was between Father's table and the long, high desk where his men stood or sat on high stools doing their books when they were not trundling boxes on a truck," writes Emily Carr in *The Book of Small.* "There was an iron safe in one corner of the office with a letterpress on top and there were two yellow chairs for customers to sit on while Father wrote their orders in his book." Shortly before his death in 1888, Carr sold his modest warehouse just to the south of this building to Robert Rithet, the businessman who owned the building next door.

EVE LAZARUS PHOTO

12) THE RITHET BUILDING

1117–1134 Wharf Street

Continue down Langley and then turn west on Fort and North at Wharf Street to see this historic area of the city. Built in 1861 and added to in 1865, 1885, and 1889, the fancy Italianate warehouse has cast-iron framing and dramatic windows for retail display. Original owner Robert P. Rithet was a partner with Robert Dunsmuir in the Albion Iron Works. The fountain in the lobby is the original Fort Victoria well that supplied scarce water to early Victoria, its commercial buildings, and the wharves in the 1860s. Historical photographs in the lobby tell the story of the area and the well, which was uncovered during renovations by the BC government in 1975.

Keep heading down Wharf Street to the Inner Harbour. You'll find many of Victoria's popular tourist attractions here. Enjoy your stroll around Downtown Victoria.

EVE LAZARUS PHOTO

Architects

FRANCIS RATTENBURY (1867–1935)

Francis Rattenbury, 25, moved to Victoria in 1892 shortly after winning a design competition for BC's Parliament Buildings against 60 other architects. Although massively over budget, the Parliament Buildings propelled the young architect's career, and before long he had a slew of buildings after his name including the Empress Hotel, the Crystal Gardens, the CPR Steamship Building, the Bank of Montreal on Government Street (1897), and the Vancouver Court House (1911), as well as his own Oak Bay mansion, *Iechinihl*, now a private school.

In 1898, Rattenbury stunned Victoria's society by marrying Florence Eleanor Nunn, the adopted daughter of a boarding-house keeper. The couple had two children: Francis born in 1899 and Mary in 1904.

Gradually, things started to unravel. Rattenbury had a falling out with the CPR and resigned as its architect. He demanded total control of his projects and would fire off pompous letters to clients who interfered with his designs. He lost a fortune in the 1913 crash. At home, things were also falling apart.

In 1923, with his career and marriage crumbling, Rattenbury met Alma Pakenham, twice-married and 30 years younger. When Florrie refused to divorce him, Rattenbury had the heat and electricity cut off at the house and scandalized Victoria's society by flaunting his affair.

When Florrie eventually agreed to a divorce, as part of the settlement Rattenbury agreed to provide her with a house of her own. In 1925, she bought a corner lot at 1513 Prospect Place. Samuel Maclure, who had worked with Rattenbury on Government House, designed Florrie's new home with a view of *Iechinihl*, where Rattenbury lived with Alma.

Florrie died in 1929, the same year that Rattenbury and Alma moved to Bournemouth, England. By all accounts the architect should have ended his life in obscurity, but Alma took up with the 18-year-old chauffeur George Stoner. In a fit of jealousy, George bashed Rattenbury to death in 1935. Both Alma and George were tried for murder, Alma was acquitted, but after hearing George would hang, she promptly stabbed herself, fell into a river, and drowned. George later had his death sentence overturned.

Francis Rattenbury, 1913.
COURTESY OAK BAY ARCHIVES

(opposite) Wharf Street from the Inner Harbour. EVE LAZARUS PHOTO

Samuel Maclure.

SAMUEL MACLURE (1860–1929)

Samuel Maclure has his fingerprints all over hundreds of buildings around British Columbia, many of which still stand. Born just outside of New Westminster, Maclure worked as a telegrapher in Vancouver before spending a year at art school and turning to architecture and setting up a practice in Victoria.

In 1885, he placed an ad on the front page of the *British Colonist* announcing that "Mr. S. Maclure (late of Spring Garden Art School, Philadelphia) is prepared to give instruction in drawing, painting in oil and satin, etc. Also instruction given in telegraphy. Residence: Blanshard and Fisgard Streets."

As well as a talented artist, Maclure had considerable design range. His buildings include the flamboyant Charles Murray Queen Anne house in New Westminster (1890), Gabriola on Davie Street in Vancouver (1901), Hatley Castle in 1925, and many other houses featured throughout this book.

Maclure was an obsessively hands-on architect. He would regularly catch the CPR midnight boat from Victoria—an eight-hour trip—to supervise his Vancouver work. He never owned a car and would travel to different job sites by street car, often reading the *Oxford Book of Verse*.

In 1899, Maclure designed the "Maclure Bungalow" at 641 Superior Street, a style of house that he became known for, and where he and wife Margaret (Daisy) lived until they moved to Oak Bay in 1906. The foundation of the house now sits somewhere under the Beacon Hill Villa, but its mate, the Arts and Crafts cottage Maclure designed at 649 Superior, is still intact and operated as a bed and breakfast. Original owner Robert Porter—a butcher who became mayor of Victoria in 1919—his wife Flora, and their six children lived there from 1896. The house stayed in the family for almost a century.

THOMAS HOOPER (1857–1935)

At one point, Thomas Hooper had the largest architectural practice in Western Canada, with offices in three cities, writes Donald Luxton in *Building the West*. Hooper designed hundreds of buildings, working first from Vancouver after his move there in 1886, and then moving to Victoria four years later.

Hooper built a house for himself and his wife Rebecca at Belleville and Menzies Street in 1900. Named Haterleigh, after his birthplace in Devon, the Arts and Crafts–style house, with its twist of Edwardian, was moved in 1911 to its present location at 243 Kingston Street, James Bay, and is now an upscale bed and breakfast.

One of Hooper's earliest commissions in Victoria is the Empire Hotel at 546 Johnson Street, designed for Alexander Milne, a collector of customs and controller of Chinese for the Port of Victoria in 1890. Completed the next year at a cost of $12,000, the Milne building was Hooper's first foray into private development and the four-storey red brick building was the scene of Charlie Kincaid's grisly murder in 1898.

Other commissions in Victoria's downtown include the Rogers' Chocolates Building on Government Street, which Hooper designed with partners Elwood Watkins and John Teague in 1903; the Munro's Books Building designed for the Royal Bank in 1909; and, oddly, Christina Haas's brothel on Cook Street in 1912. Also in 1912 he completed work on Hycroft, A.D. McRae's magnificent Shaughnessy mansion, and the year in which Hooper drew an elaborate submission for the new University of British Columbia (although he did not win the commission).

Things started to go downhill for the architect when the economy disintegrated in 1913. Soon after, he moved to New York but failed to revive his career. Hooper, writes Luxton, returned penniless to Vancouver in 1927, where he died in an old folks' home in 1935.

Thomas Hooper, 1905.

Bibliography

BOOKS

Adams, John. (2002). *Ghosts and Legends of Bastion Square*. Victoria: Discover the Past.

Amos, Robert. (2007). *Artists in Their Studios*. Victoria: Touchwood Editions.

Appleton, Thomas E. (1968). *Usque ad Mare. A History of the Canadian Coast Guard and Marine Services*. Ottawa: Department of Transport.

Belyk, Robert C. (2001). *Great Shipwrecks of the Pacific Coast*. Toronto: John Wiley & Sons.

Bingham, Janet. (1985). *Samuel Maclure*. Victoria: Horsdal & Schubart.

Birnie, Lisa Hobbs. (1996). *Western Lights: Fourteen Distinctive British Columbians*. Vancouver: Raincoast Books.

Blanchet, M. Wylie. (2011). *The Curve of Time* (50th anniversary edition). Vancouver: Whitecap.

Bovey, Patricia E. (1996). *A Passion for Art: The Art and Dynamics of the Limners*. Victoria: Sono Nis Press.

Carr, Emily. (1993). *The Complete Writings of Emily Carr*. Vancouver: Douglas & McIntyre.

Cash, Gwen. (1977). *Off the Record: The Personal Reminiscences of Canada's First Woman Reporter*. Langley: Stagecoach.

Castle, Geoffrey (Ed.). (1989). *Saanich, An Illustrated History*. Corporation of the District of Saanich.

Castle, Geoffrey, & Green, Valerie, eds. (2006). *Saanich Centennial, 1906–2006: 100 Years, 100 Stories*. Corporation of the District of Saanich.

Chamberlain, Paul G. (2000). *The Dingle House: A Century of Ghosts, Kings and Celebrities*. Victoria: Dingle House Press.

Converse, Cathy. (2008). *Following the Curve of Time*. Victoria: Touchwood Editions.

Duffus, Maureen. (1993). *Craigflower Country: A History of View Royal 1850–1950*. View Royal Historical Committee.

Eaton, Leonard, K. (1971). *The Architecture of Samuel Maclure*. Victoria: Art Gallery of Greater Victoria.

Eversole, Linda J. (2005). *Stella: Unrepentant Madam*. Victoria: Touchwood Editions.

Field, Dorothy. (1984). *Built Heritage in Esquimalt: An Inventory*. Victoria: B.C. Heritage Trust.

Forbes, Elizabeth. (1971). *Wild Roses at Their Feet: Pioneer Women of Vancouver Island*. BC Centennial 1971 Committee.

Foster, David. (2008). *Hitman: Forty Years Making Music, Topping Charts & Winning Grammys*. New York: Pocket Books.

Gordon, Katherine. (2002). *A Curious Life: The Biography of Princess Peggy Abkhazi*. Winlaw: Sono Nis Press

Gosnell, R.E. (1906). *History of British Columbia*. Victoria: Lewis Publishing.

Gray, Charlotte. (2008). *Nellie McClung*. Toronto: Penguin Canada.

Gray, Larry. (2010). *A Heritage Gem: The House That Captured the Innkeepers*. Victoria: Cricket Publishing.

Green, Valerie. (2001). *Victoria's Houses from the Past*. Victoria: Touchwood Editions.

Gregson, Harry. (1970). *A History of Victoria 1842–1970*. Victoria: Victoria Observer Publishing.

Hembroff-Schleicher, Edythe (1978). *Emily Carr: The Untold Story*. Surrey: Hancock House.

Humphreys, Danda. (1999). *On the Street Where You Live: Pioneer Pathways of Early Victoria*. Surrey: Heritage House.

Hustak, Alan. (1998). *Titanic: Canadian Story*. Montreal: Vehicule Press.

Hutchison, Bruce. (1976). *The Far Side of the Street*. Toronto: MacMillan of Canada.

Hutchison, Bruce. (1988). *A Life in the Country*. Vancouver: Douglas & McIntyre.

Iglauer, Edith. (1991). *The Strangers Next Door*. Madiera Park: Harbour Publishing.

Kupecek, Linda. (2003). *Rebel Women: Achievements Beyond the Ordinary*. Victoria: Altitude Publishing.

Lindberg, Ted. (1991). *A Portrait of Myfanwy*. Victoria: Morriss Publishing.

Luxton, Donald (Ed.) (2003). *Building the West: The Early Architects of British Columbia*. Vancouver: Talonbooks.

Luxton, Donald (Ed.) with Jennifer Nell Barr. (2008). *Saanich Heritage Register*. Corporation of the District of Saanich.

Luxton, Norman. (1971). *Tilikum: Luxton's Pacific Crossing*. Sidney: Gray's Publishing.

McClung, Nellie. (2003). *The Complete Autobiography*. Peterborough: Broadview Press.

Mason, Adrienne. (2003). *Tales from the West Coast*. Victoria: Amazing Stories.

Minaker, D.W. (1998). *The Gorge of Summers Gone: A History of Victoria's Inland Waterway*. D.W. Minaker.

Munro, Sheila. (2001). *Lives of Mothers and Daughters*. Toronto: McClelland & Stewart.

Obee, David. (2008). *Making the News: A Times Colonist Look at 150 Years of History*. Victoria Times Colonist.

O'Keefe, Betty, & Macdonald, Ian. (1998). *The Final Voyage of the Princess Sophia: Did They All Have to Die?* Victoria: Heritage House.

Parker, Marion, & Tyrrell, Robert. (1995). *Rumrunner: The Life and Times of Johnny Schnarr*. Victoria: Orca Books.

Reksten, Terry. (1986). *More English Than the English: A Very Social History of Victoria*. Victoria: Orca Books.

Reksten, Terry. (1998). *Rattenbury*. Victoria: Sono Nis Press.

Savage, Candace. (1979). *Our Nell: A Scrapbook Biography of Nellie L. McClung*. Halifax: Goodread Biographies.

Scott, Bruce R. (1970). *Breakers Ahead! A History of Shipwrecks on the Graveyard of the Pacific*. Sidney: Review Publishing.

Segger, Martin. (1986). *The Buildings of Samuel Maclure*. Victoria: Sono Nis Press.

Shipman, Nell. (1987). *The Silent Screen and My Talking Heart*. Boise: Boise State University.

Skelton, Robin. (1979). *Herbert Siebner, A Monograph*. Victoria: Sono Nis Press.

Skelton, Robin. (1988). *The Memoirs of a Literary Blockhead*. Toronto: MacMillan of Canada.

Skelton, Robin, & Kozocari, Jean. (1989). *A Gathering of Ghosts: Haunting and Exorcisms*. Saskatoon: Western Producer Prairie Books.

Spaner, David. (2003). *Dreaming in the Rain*. Vancouver: Arsenal Pulp Press.

Sparks, Jean. (1940). *Oak Bay, British Columbia: In Photographs*. Corporation of the District of Oak Bay.

Starkins, Edward. (2011). *Who Killed Janet Smith?* Vancouver: Anvil Press.

Tippett, Maria. (1979). *Emily Carr: A Biography*. Toronto: Oxford University Press.

Victoria Heritage Foundation. (2004–2009). *This Old House*, Volumes 1–4. City of Victoria.

Voss, John C. (1976). *The Venturesome Voyages of Captain Voss*. Sidney: Gray's Publishing.

Walbran, Captain John T. (1909). *British Columbia Coast Names: Their Origin and History*. Ottawa: Government Printing Bureau.

NEWSPAPERS AND MAGAZINES

British Colonist, BC Motorist, BC Studies, Columbian, Daily Colonist, Gardens West, Goldstream News Gazette, Maclean's, New York Times, Oak Bay News, Outdoor Ideas & Solutions, Province, Saanich News, Saturday Night, Vancouver Sun, Victoria Daily Colonist, Washington Times, Whitehorse Star, World

WEBSITES

ABCbookworld.com

Airing Victoria's Dirty Laundry: http://web.uvic.ca/vv/student/airingvictorias/index.html

bcassessment.ca

conservancy.bc.ca

Patrick Dunae's Geographies of Sexual Commerce in Victoria, British Columbia, 1862-1912, Department of History, Vancouver Island University: http://www.cliomedia.ca/Dunae-CHA60.pdf

encyclopedia-titanica.org/

genealogysearch.org/Canada/british-columbia.html

heritageoakbay.ca

historicplaces.ca

myEsquimalt.com

oakbayvillage.ca

recreatingeden.com

Vancouver Public Library, city directories: vpl.ca/bccd/index.php

Victoriangardentours.com

victoriasvictoria.ca, an online index to Historical Newspapers in Victoria. Victoria's Victoria 2007 Leona Taylor and Dorothy Mindenhall.

Index